NATURAL RESOURCES

Plants

NATURAL RESOURCES

AGRICULTURE
ANIMALS
ENERGY
FORESTS
LANDS
MINERALS
PLANTS
WATER AND ATMOSPHERE

PLANTS

LIFE FROM THE EARTH

Julie Kerr Casper, Ph.D.

CHELSEA HOUSE
PUBLISHERS
An imprint of Infobase Publishing

Plants

Copyright © 2007 by Infobase Publishing

All rights reserved. No part of this book may be reproduced or utilized in any form or by any means, electronic or mechanical, including photocopying, recording, or by any information storage or retrieval systems, without permission in writing from the publisher. For information contact:

Chelsea House
An imprint of Infobase Publishing
132 West 31st Street
New York, NY 10001

ISBN-10: 0-8160-6358-3
ISBN-13: 978-0-8160-6358-1

Library of Congress Cataloging-in-Publication Data

Casper, Julie Kerr.
  Plants : life from the earth / Julie Kerr Casper.
  p. cm.—(Natural resources)
  Includes bibliographical references and index.
  ISBN 0-8160-6358-3 (hardcover)
  1. Botany. 2. Plants. I. Title. II. Series: Natural resources (New York, N.Y.)
  QK45.2.C38 2007
  581.6'3—dc22   2006028965

Chelsea House books are available at special discounts when purchased in bulk quantities for businesses, associations, institutions, or sales promotions. Please call our Special Sales Department in New York at (212) 967-8800 or (800) 322-8755.

You can find Chelsea House on the World Wide Web at http://www.chelseahouse.com

Text design by Erik Lindstrom
Cover design by Ben Peterson

Printed in the United States of America

Bang NMSG 10 9 8 7 6 5 4 3 2 1

This book is printed on acid-free paper.

All links and Web addresses were checked and verified to be correct at the time of publication. Because of the dynamic nature of the Web, some addresses and links may have changed since publication and may no longer be valid.

Contents

Preface   vi

Acknowledgments   x

Introduction   xi

1 | Concepts of Botany   1

2 | The Evolution and Adaptation of Plants   30

3 | Renewable and Nonrenewable Resources   42

4 | Development of Botanical Resources   57

5 | Uses of Botanical Resources   75

6 | The Importance of Plants   92

7 | Management of Plants in a Rapidly Changing World   115

8 | Conservation of Critical Botanical Systems   134

9 | Conclusions: Future Issues and Discoveries   152

Appendix   166

Glossary   168

Further Reading   179

Index   187

PREFACE

Mankind did not weave the web of life.
We are but one strand in it. Whatever we
do to the web, we do to ourselves . . .
All things are bound together.

—Chief Seattle

The Earth has been blessed with an abundant supply of natural resources. Natural resources are those elements that exist on the planet for the use and benefit of all living things. Scientists commonly divide them down into distinct groups for the purposes of studying them. These groups include agricultural resources, plants, animals, energy sources, landscapes, forests, minerals, and water and atmospheric resources.

One thing we humans have learned is that many of the important resources we have come to depend on are not renewable. *Nonrenewable* means that once a resource is depleted it is gone forever. The fossil fuel that gasoline is produced from is an example of a nonrenewable resource. There is only a finite supply, and once it is used up, that is the end of it.

While living things such as animals are typically considered renewable resources, meaning they can potentially be replenished, animals hunted to extinction become nonrenewable resources. As we know from past evidence, the extinctions of the dinosaurs, the woolly mammoth, and the saber-toothed tiger were complete. Sometimes, extinctions like this may be caused by natural factors, such as climate change, drought, or flood, but many extinctions are caused by the activities of humans.

Overhunting caused the extinction of the passenger pigeon, which was once plentiful throughout North America. The bald eagle was hunted to the brink of extinction before it became a protected species, and African elephants are currently threatened with extinction because they are still being hunted for their ivory tusks. Overhunting is only one potential threat, though. Humans are also responsible for habitat loss. When humans change land use and convert an animal's habitat to a city, this destroys the animal's living space and food sources and promotes its endangerment.

Plants can also be endangered or become extinct. An important issue facing us today is the destruction of the Earth's tropical rain forests. Scientists believe there may be medicinal value in many plant species that have not been discovered yet. Therefore, destroying a plant species could be destroying a medical benefit for the future.

Because of human impact and influence all around the Earth, it is important to understand our natural resources, protect them, use them wisely, and plan for future generations. The environment—land, soil, water, plants, minerals, and animals—is a marvelously complex and dynamic system that often changes in ways too subtle to perceive. Today, we have enlarged our vision of the landscape with which we interact. Farmers manage larger units of land, which makes their job more complex. People travel greater distances more frequently. Even when they stay at home, they experience and affect a larger share of the world through electronic communications and economic activities— and natural resources have made these advancements possible.

The pace of change in our society has accelerated as well. New technologies are always being developed. Many people no longer spend all their time focused in one place or using things in traditional ways. People now move from one place to another and are constantly developing and using new and different resources.

A sustainable society requires a sustainable environment. Because of this, we must think of natural resources in new ways. Today, more than ever, we must dedicate our efforts to conserve the land. We still live in a beautiful, largely natural world, but that world is quickly changing. World population growth and our desire to live comfortably are exerting pressures on our soil, air, water, and other natural resources. As we destroy and fragment natural habitats, we continue to push nonhuman life into ever-smaller pockets. Today, we run the risk of those places becoming isolated islands on a domesticated landscape.

In order to be responsible caretakers of the planet, it is important to realize that we humans have a partnership with the Earth and the other life that shares the planet with us. This series presents a refreshing and informative way to view the Earth's natural resources. *Agriculture: The Food We Grow and Animals We Raise* looks at agricultural resources to see how responsible conservation, such as caring for the soil, will give us continued food to feed growing populations. *Plants: Life From the Earth* examines the multitude of plants that exist and the role they play in biodiversity. The use of plants in medicines and in other products that people use every day is also covered.

In *Animals: Creatures That Roam the Planet,* the series focuses on the diverse species of animals that live on the planet, including the important roles they have played in the advancement of civilization. This book in the series also looks at habitat destruction, exotic species, animals that are considered in danger of extinction, and how people can help to keep the environment intact.

Next, in *Energy: Powering the Past, Present, and Future,* the series explores the Earth's energy resources—such as renewable power from water, ocean energy, solar energy, wind energy, and biofuels; and non-renewable sources from oil shale, tar sands, and fossil fuels. In addition, the future of energy and high-tech inventions on the horizon are also explored.

In *Lands: Taming the Wilds,* the series addresses the land and how civilizations have been able to tame deserts, mountains, arctic regions, forests, wetlands, and floodplains. The effects that our actions can have on the landscape for years to come are also explored. In *Forests: More Than Just Trees,* the series examines the Earth's forested areas and how unique and important these areas are to medicine, construction, recreation, and commercial products. The effects of deforestation, pest outbreaks, and wildfires—and how these can impact people for generations to come—are also addressed.

In *Minerals: Gifts From the Earth*, the bounty of minerals in the Earth and the discoveries scientists have made about them are examined. Moreover, this book in the series gives an overview of the critical part minerals play in many common activities and how they affect our lives every day.

Finally, in *Water and Atmosphere: The Lifeblood of Natural Systems*, the series looks at water and atmospheric resources to find out just how these resources are the lifeblood of the natural system—from drinking water, food production, and nutrient storage to recreational values. Drought, sea-level rise, soil management, coastal development, the effects of air and water pollution, and deep-sea exploration and what it holds for the future are also explored.

The reader will learn the wisdom of recycling, reducing, and reusing our natural resources, as well as discover many simple things that can be done to protect the environment. Practical approaches such as not leaving the water running while brushing your teeth, turning the lights off when leaving a room, using reusable cloth bags to transport groceries, building a backyard wildlife refuge, planting a tree, forming a carpool, or starting a local neighborhood recycling program are all explored.

Everybody is somebody's neighbor, and shared responsibility is the key to a healthy environment. The cheapest—and most effective—conservation comes from working with nature. This series presents things that people can do for the environment now and the important role we all can play for the future. As a wise Native-American saying goes, "We do not inherit the Earth from our ancestors—we borrow it from our children."

ACKNOWLEDGMENTS

While plants surround us and we use them every day, many people are not aware of just how much we depend on plant life. Plants play a critical role in everyone's existence. Some uses may be obvious—such as for sources of food. Other uses may be more subtle—such as for the experimentation and manufacture of medicines.

I hope to instill in you—the reader—an understanding and appreciation of plant life and its role in our environment. Perhaps raising awareness of plants and all they do and have to offer will "plant the seeds" of conservation with regard to this precious resource and cultivate the desire to protect it and use it wisely.

I would sincerely like to thank several of the federal government agencies that study, manage, protect, and preserve plant life—in particular, the U.S. Department of Agriculture (USDA), the Agricultural Research Service (ARS), the Natural Resources Conservation Service (NRCS), the National Park Service (NPS), the U.S. Forest Service (USFS), and the Bureau of Land Management (BLM) for providing an abundance of resources on this important subject. I would also like to acknowledge and give thanks to the many universities across the country and their botany departments, as well as private organizations that diligently strive to protect our natural resources, such as the World Wildlife Fund.

INTRODUCTION

Over millions of years, plants have adapted to the various environments on Earth. They can grow nearly everywhere—even in places where animals have a hard time surviving. In fact, the only places plants cannot grow are on the polar ice caps, on the tops of the highest mountains, and at the bottom of the deepest oceans.

Plant life is crucial—all life on Earth depends on plants in some way. Even carnivorous animals—animals that only eat other animals—rely on plants to feed their prey. Plants are the basis of all food chains on Earth, making even the largest meat-eating animals dependent on plants.

Sometimes humans think that they are the most important living things on Earth, but they are not. If humans ceased to exist, life on the planet would go on. But, if all the green plants disappeared, everything but a few bacteria would eventually die off, and the composition of Earth's atmosphere would change, making Earth very different from what it is today.

There are about 380,000 different species of plants in the world. Botanists—scientists who study plants—believe there are probably thousands more to be discovered. The range of plant life is enormous—from tiny algae that float in the sea and freshwater and consist of just one cell, to the beautiful flowering plants and giant trees, like the redwoods in California.

This volume in the Natural Resources series focuses on the many aspects that make plants such a valuable resource. Chapter 1 discusses the role of biodiversity, the major biomes of Earth, the life cycles of plants, and the many unique ways plants have adapted to their environment. Chapter 2 looks at the evolution of plants and what kind of environment may have existed during the age of the dinosaurs. It addresses the reasons why some plants have become extinct and others have not.

Chapter 3 examines the various resources provided by plants, both renewable and nonrenewable. It also addresses the crucial resource cycles that healthy plant communities depend on, such as the water cycle, nitrogen cycle, and carbon cycle.

Chapter 4 explores the development of botanical resources. It looks at the many mechanisms that plants have developed in order to survive. It reveals the ingenious ways that different seeds are disbursed to increase plants' chances for future survival. It also looks at how certain species become isolated and are found only in one specific area of the world. Finally, it introduces the reader to the unusual field of ethnobotany and why many types of plants are culturally significant to different groups of people throughout the world.

Chapter 5 examines the many uses of plants, such as their scientific applications, food value, use in building shelter, critical role in medicine and health care, how they are used to generate energy and produce many industrial products, as well as how plants provide people with inspirational benefits.

Chapter 6 discusses the importance of plants and the goods and services they provide to communities every day. It examines crossbreeding and plant genetics and why those scientific fields are so important. It identifies the role plants have in our recreational opportunities, their effects on animal habitat, their use in wilderness survival, and the important—and often surprising—role plants have played in civilizations throughout history. The current ecological issues we face are also examined.

Chapter 7 shows the reader how this important resource is being managed today in a rapidly changing world. It discusses habitat destruction and loss, as well as the effects of disease, pollution, overexploitation, and poor land-management practices. It also discusses poisonous plants and the importance of plant identification and safety.

Chapter 8 presents the most crucial conservation issues that face natural resource managers today and how they are being dealt with. This chapter looks at concepts like wilderness and environmental protection, endangered plants and what that means, and which species are disappearing at an alarming rate. It also shows the reader how everyone can become a "backyard conservationist" and help protect plants.

Finally, Chapter 9 covers future issues and scientific discoveries that show how plants are constantly improving our standard of living. It looks at biotechnology, the important role of seed banks, new developments and experiments, and even how plants are being used in outer space. It also looks at humans' role in the big picture and covers things we all can do to help the environment.

CONCEPTS OF BOTANY

From the smallest **flowers** to the tallest trees, the life cycles of plants are made up of the same stages. Seeds sprout into **seedlings**, which grow and produce **leaves** and **stems** or woody trunks. Eventually, they produce flowers and **seeds** of their own, and the cycle repeats itself for the next generation. This chapter addresses the role of biodiversity, the major **biomes** of Earth, the life cycles of plants, why plants grow in specific biomes, as well as plant **adaptations** and their mechanisms of survival.

THE ROLE OF BIODIVERSITY

Diversity and adaptation are crucial to a plant's existence, just as they are to the existence of humans. If a plant cannot adapt to an **environment**, it will not survive. Diversity extends from one spectrum to another. One of the smallest plants is duckweed—about the size of a pinhead. Giant sequoias, on the other hand, are among the world's tallest trees (trees are plants with a single woody stem called a trunk). The largest known sequoia is in California, known by the name William T. Sherman, named after a famous army officer in the Civil War. The base of the trunk is 36 feet (11 meters) across. The tree is more than 272 feet (83 m) high. It weighs more than 6,000 tons (5,000 metric tons), and is about 3,500 years old.

The largest redwood tree, also found in California, measures 385 feet (117 m) high—as high as a 38-story skyscraper. The tree with the largest spread is the banyan. As a banyan grows, **roots** begin to grow down from the branches like wooden pillars. When they reach the ground, they grow into the soil and become secondary tree trunks. A single banyan tree can have hundreds of these stiltlike supports, enabling it to spread over large areas. The largest flower in the world is the rafflesia. Found in Southeast Asia, the plant lives mainly underground and survives by stealing food from the roots of other plants. Its flower, however, forms above ground and can grow to 4 feet (1.3 m) across and can weigh 25 pounds (11 kilograms). The flower has a pungent odor—it smells like rotting meat.

The largest leaves belong to the raffia palms in Africa. Its leaves can grow to 65 feet (20 m) long. The Victoria water lily in South America has leaves that are more than 6 feet (2 m) across. They are sturdy enough to float a small child.

Plant biodiversity is important because it helps make all ecosystems more stable and better living environments for all **species** of animals. There are many benefits of biodiversity. For example, in forests, scientists believe there are cures for diseases that have not yet been found. Therefore, if biodiversity is reduced, the chance of discovering lifesaving drugs may be lost. Without biodiversity, soil formation processes, air and water purification, and all the crucial resource cycles—such as the nitrogen cycle and carbon cycle—would be jeopardized. The elimination of one component causes a ripple effect that impacts all the other components. This is detrimental since all forms of life are dependent on working resource cycles.

When **botanists** study biodiversity, they gather field information in order to inventory what plants exist. Because it would be too difficult,

A giant sequoia in Northern California, affectionately named General Grant, located in Sequoia National Park. *(Courtesy of the National Park Service)*

Victoria water lilies in South America can grow more than six feet across. These, located in Oahu, Hawaii, are five feet (1.5 m) in diameter. *(Courtesy of U.S. National Oceanic and Atmospheric Administration; photo by Commander John Bortniak)*

expensive, and time-consuming to inventory every square inch of an area, botanists take representative field samples. Using this method, they inventory a scattering of representative field plots located within the study region. Because these individual sites—which can be linear transects (strips of area) or block areas—represent what plant life lives in the area, botanists can use this data to make projections about the numbers of each plant in the entire region. This allows scientists to get an understanding of an area's degree of biodiversity.

There are several advantages of having diverse plant life in a **habitat**. For example, a greater variety of plants provides **nutrients** to a greater variety of insects. If a disease strikes one plant, other plant species will survive. Because of this, botanists use biodiversity as an indicator of the environment's health.

On a global scale, some areas are more diverse that others. Tropical **rain forests** have the greatest number of species of any biome. Scientists believe that 50% of all known species on Earth are found in the tropical rain forests. Interestingly, however, rain forests only cover about 6% of the world's land surface. Because of this, it has caused great environmental concern that rain forests are being destroyed at alarming rates. It is quite possible that purposely lowering the level of biodiversity could jeopardize finding future cures for many serious diseases, such as cancer.

Earth supports many different habitats—or biomes—each of which has distinct features and distinct plant and animal populations. Animals and plants are adapted to the conditions of the habitats in which they live. These specialized adaptations help plants survive in the specific environments they are found in. For example, in the tundra—which is a cold arctic climate—vegetation can only survive if it grows low to the ground—hence the reason why tall trees do not grow there.

Plants near oceans have adapted to being able to tolerate higher concentrations of salt. **Desert** plants have developed characteristics to deal with the heat and lack of water. For example, cacti have the ability to fill up with water during rainstorms and then store the excess water for long periods of time in order to survive during drought cycles. Seeds can also remain dormant for long periods of time. Once environmental conditions are adequate for survival, seeds will germinate, and flowers will bloom for short periods of time.

Biomes are influenced by abiotic factors (the nonliving parts of the ecosystem) such as annual rainfall, average daily or monthly temperature, temperature extremes, and seasonal changes. These abiotic factors have a direct influence on the biotic factors of an ecosystem—the living parts, such as plants and animals.

Of the 380,000 current species of plants, flowering plants dominate the classification. There are roughly 250,000 species of flowering plants.

The remainders are mainly conifers, **ferns**, and **mosses**. Each species has its unique characteristics, use, and importance to humankind.

BIOMES OF EARTH

There are several different biomes on Earth. Rather than having distinct boundaries, they transition from one to another depending where on the planet they are located. For example, the tropical rain forests are found at Earth's equator. The climate at the equator is warm and wet, enabling a large variety of species to grow there. The vegetation is so dense that the rain forests consist of several layers, or *canopies*. Dense vegetation grows at ground level, and above that are shrubs at different heights and then above that are species of trees that occupy different heights in the forest. Here the vegetation is so thick that the ground is often dark from lack of sunlight filtering down to the lower levels of the forest.

Moving north, Earth's climate is cooler with warm, wet summers and cold winters. Temperate forests grow in these regions. There are fewer species of vegetation in temperate forests, but there are larger populations of each species. In temperate forests, the **deciduous trees** shed their leaves in the fall. In addition to trees, there are also shrubs, grasses, ferns, and wildflowers.

Further north are the **coniferous** forests. These areas have cold winters, but the **evergreen** trees do not shed their leaves (or pine needles). Evergreens are able to survive because their needles have a small surface area and are coated with a thick layer of wax. There are fewer species in coniferous forests.

Moving still further north toward the North Pole, the tundra has long, cold winters and short cool summers. Grasses, **lichens**, sedges, and small shrubs grow in the tundra.

Plant communities are also governed by the humidity (the amount of water vapor in the air) of a region. In more moist areas, grasslands grow. Deserts are found in drier areas.

There are many habitats in addition to forests. Each habitat type has distinct characteristics, as described below.

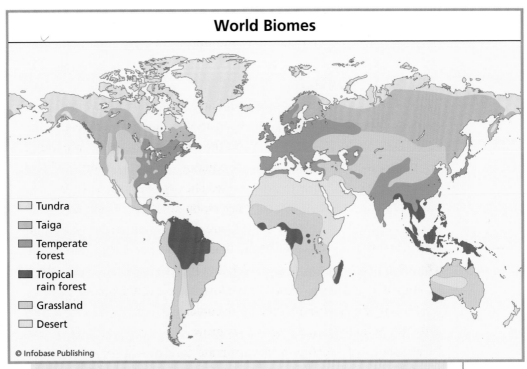

World Biomes

Tundra
Taiga
Temperate forest
Tropical rain forest
Grassland
Desert

© Infobase Publishing

The major biomes of the Earth. Each biome is associated with specific plants.

Seashore

Seashore environments can be very harsh. Not only are the air and water salty, but strong, persistent winds blow across the sand dunes adjacent to the water. Plants that live on a rocky seashore must be hearty enough to withstand water constantly splashing against them. They are also exposed to the sun and must therefore be able to survive hot, exposed conditions. Because the environment is harsh, plants have adapted to survive. Some have developed the ability to cling to rocky ledges; others have developed long **taproots** in order to reach freshwater. Some have leaves that have **evolved** to withstand persistent winds. Plants have also adapted to the salty conditions by storing groundwater in their thick, fleshy leaves. Still others have adapted to be able to grow in sandy soil that does not contain a lot of nutrients.

Ponds, Rivers, and Lakes

Because ponds are shallow bodies of water, light is able to filter to the bottom. Pond water is generally warm and contains a high level of nutrients. Several types of plants have adapted to live in ponds and fill an important role in supporting the animal life in the pond. Different plants live in different areas of the pond. Some live at the edge, some float on the surface, and others live entirely underwater. Plants such as cattail, which grow along the edges of ponds and lakes, play a significant role in stabilizing the shoreline. Their roots help trap soil along the shore. Many plant species that grow along the shores, such as rushes, reeds, and grass, provide critical habitat for birds to build nests in. **Algae** are often found within the pond. Although algae do not have stems, leaves, or roots, they have **chlorophyll** and can make their own food. Underwater plants, such as pondweed, add **oxygen** to the water, which benefits fish, frogs, and other pond and lake wildlife.

Different plants also grow in different places along a river. For example, moss grows in the shade in areas that are moist. Other plants, such as the marsh violet, trap soil and mud along the riverbank, stabilizing the bank and providing homes for tiny animals. Riparian (river) vegetation also provides critical habitat for birds and other animals.

Wetlands

Over thousands of years, lakes can change into wetlands, a transitional environment between land and water. Rivers that flow into the lake deposit sediment. As the lake bed slowly rises, the water becomes shallower. The land plants take root in the silt at the shoreline. Water plants gradually grow toward the center of the lake, allowing more silt to build up. Eventually, **peat** forms under the marsh, allowing even more plants to take hold.

Wetland soils are usually soggy and flooded. Wetland areas include marshes, swamps, and **bogs**. The plants in wetlands have adapted to grow partly in and partly out of the water. Some have adapted to float on the surface of the water, while others live completely underwater.

A saguaro cactus near Phoenix, Arizona, towers toward the sky. These cacti grow very slowly and can live more than 100 years. *(Photo by Jerel G. Casper, Nature's Images)*

Plants along the bank provide food and shelter for animals. Wetlands are fragile environments and are increasingly threatened by human activities. Water **pollution**, drainage, trampling, and destruction of wetlands have caused many wetland plants to become **extinct**.

Desert

The lack of water and intense daytime heat are the main problems for plants that grow in the desert. In order to survive, the roots of desert plants grow deep into the ground or spread out widely in search of water. Because rainfall is sporadic, desert plants have learned to adapt by storing water. Desert plants can store water in their roots, in **succulent** leaves, or in ridges that can expand to hold it. The giant saguaro cactus is an example of a plant that can hold great quantities of water.

The fleshy ridges are able to hold water and expand. As the saguaro uses the water, the pleats contract. A saguaro can store enough water to last nearly three years without rainfall.

Many desert plants have developed waxy leaves in order to conserve water. Cacti have spines, which evolved to reduce the amount of water lost through **transpiration**. The sharp spines on other cacti reflect and scatter the fierce rays of the sun. In areas where the soil is salty, sage-brush has adapted to survive those conditions. Sagebrush provides an important food source for many desert animals.

Arctic

In the Arctic tundra, the soil is permanently frozen. This means that when temperatures warm up enough to melt snow and ice, the water cannot penetrate the frozen soil, so it gathers on top, creating vast areas of stagnant water. Some tundra plants have adapted to these soggy conditions. At the tree line, the trees are often bare on the windblown side. Low-growing flowering plants, mosses, lichens, and grasses can survive near ground level because the temperature is warmer, and the wind less frigid.

Grasslands

Grasslands form in areas that get more rain than deserts but less rain than forests. There are not many trees in these areas. Grasses are much hardier, and they lose less water in dry winds than taller plants. There is an abundance of grasses that have adapted to grassland environments. Grasslands are ideal habitats for many types of grazing animals. Grasses can continue to grow—even when grazed—because the growing **cells** are at the base of the grass instead of in the leaves.

Grasses play a critical part in the life of many other life-forms. Grasses are one of the world's most important plant types. They provide food for most domesticated and wild animals. They are the source of most of the world's sugar (from sugarcane). All the cereal crops, such as wheat, oats, rye, barley, millet, rice, and corn are also grown in the grasslands. The world's largest grasslands are the veldts of South

Africa, the pampas of South America, the steppes of central Asia, and the prairies of North America.

The types of plants that can grow in grasslands vary according to the soil type of the region. Soils that are alkaline and rich in **minerals** can support a bigger variety of species than those grasslands that contain acidic soils.

Tropics

Tropical areas are characterized by hot, humid weather, with virtually no seasonal changes. Daytime temperatures usually exceed 80°F (27°C), and rainfall is usually greater than 80 inches (203 centimeters). These conditions are ideal for plant growth, which is why there is such a diverse range of vegetation in tropical areas.

The favorable conditions of the tropics encourages the evolution of new plant species. Besides having several canopies of vegetation, there is also diverse plant life, such as climbing plants, called lianas. Lianas climb up the trees and extend throughout the various canopies. Some of the climbers are so strong, however, that they strangle—and eventually kill—the trees around which they have become entwined.

Some of the plants that live in the trees (such as orchids and ferns) do not have roots anchored in the ground. Instead, they dangle off the tree branches and absorb minerals and small amounts of water from the **decaying** remains of leaves and other plant material on the bark of the host tree.

The subtropics are similar to the tropics, except that they receive less rainfall and experience seasonal changes. Tropical and subtropical areas are being threatened by having the trees cut down and the land used instead for agriculture, roads, houses, and other buildings.

THE LIFE CYCLE OF A PLANT

Although various species of plants may look very different from each other, the life cycle of a plant is consistent. All plants need water, sunshine, minerals, warmth, oxygen, and **carbon dioxide** in order to grow well. Green plants make food by combining carbon dioxide from the air and water from the surrounding soil in a process called **photosynthesis**. Sunlight is the energy source that makes photosynthesis possible. A chemical in the plant—a green **pigment** called chlorophyll—traps the sun's energy and releases it, causing a chemical change.

When carbon dioxide and water are combined, they produce a sugar called **glucose**. The plant does not need the oxygen from the water, so it is expelled from the plant as a waste product. The glucose stores energy from the sun, which the plant uses to collect salts from the soil and to grow. The glucose that is not used is converted into **starch**. The plant can store the starch to use later as a food source.

During the growth cycle of a plant, the roots, leaves, stems, and flowers all have specific functions. The roots play a crucial role in a plant's existence. They consist of an underground network that spreads through the soil. The roots anchor the plant firmly in the ground. Water and dissolved minerals from the soil—such as nitrates, phosphates, and potassium—enter the roots through the tiny root hairs on the root tips. The more roots a plant has, the more water and minerals it can take in.

Roots grow into the ground, pulled down by the force of **gravity**. This response to gravity is controlled by a chemical called **auxin**, which is made by cells in the tips of the roots. The response of plants to gravity is called **geotropism**. Roots grow toward the pull of gravity (positive geotropism), and the stems grow away from it (negative geotropism).

There is a vascular system of two types of small tubes in the root called **xylem** and **phloem**. These tubes are grouped in the center of the root. Water and minerals are drawn into the root through the root hairs and then *up* the xylem to the leaves. The plant's food—glucose (sugar)—is made in the leaves. It passes *down* the phloem to the growing cells at the tips of the roots where it is used to make **cellulose** for the new cell walls.

Roots also act as a food store. Throughout the summer growing season, the plant produces more sugar than it needs. When the sugar is subsequently turned into starch, it is stored in the underground stems and roots. It stores this starch during the dormant winter months and

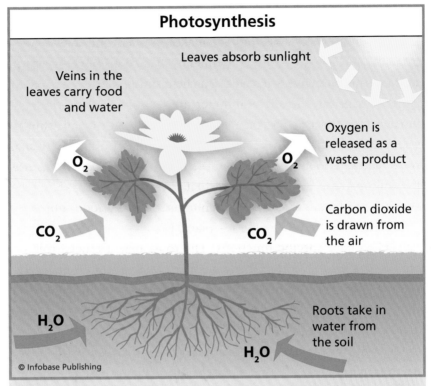

Photosynthesis

Leaves absorb sunlight

Veins in the leaves carry food and water

Oxygen is released as a waste product

O_2

O_2

CO_2

Carbon dioxide is drawn from the air

CO_2

H_2O

Roots take in water from the soil

H_2O

© Infobase Publishing

The process a plant goes through in order to produce its own food. Carbon dioxide and water combine to make glucose, while oxygen is released as a waste product. Glucose stores energy from the sun and provides food for the plant.

then uses it the following spring as a food reserve. This food reserve is what provides energy for new buds to begin growing.

There are two basic types of roots: **fibrous roots** and taproots. Fibrous roots grow from the stem of the plant and branch out in a dense network of roots. Some of these are side roots, which spread out laterally in search of water and nutrients. They also function to support the plant. Grasses have a fibrous root system. A taproot is a long root that burrows down into the soil to anchor the plant and search for water during droughts. Carrots and turnips are examples of taproots. Some plants have taproots as well as fibrous root systems.

The ends of each root have tough skin on them for protection as they burrow through the soil. When water enters the soil, minerals from the soil particles are dissolved. The water and minerals are the nutrients the plant needs to grow. They pass through the root hairs into larger passageways. They travel through these passageways and supply nutrients to other parts of the plant.

Some specialized roots grow above ground. For example, buttress roots are huge roots that grow out of the trunks of some rain forest trees. Prop roots on cornstalks are another type of root that grows above ground level in order to support the heavy stalk.

Aerial roots, another type of root, begin high up on a plant and dangle in the air, unattached. They take in water vapor from the air around it. **Rhizome** and runner roots that develop from underground stems are what allow a plant to reproduce without seeds. Examples of these types of roots are some grasses, blackberries, buttercups, spider plants, and strawberries.

Adventitious roots are additional roots produced from a stem. An example of this is the mangrove (a plant that grows in estuaries), which has roots that grow above the water in order to absorb oxygen from the air.

Leaves

A leaf is constructed from layers of cells, each layer having its own function. Leaves come in a huge range of sizes and shapes, but they all have the same function: to make food.

Plants also breathe through their leaves, a process called **respiration,** and lose water vapor through them, a process called transpiration. In flowering plants, leaves grow in two basic arrangements: (1) simple leaves with single leaf blades and (2) compound leaves with lots of small leaves clustered on one stalk. Leaves vary from plant to plant—representing natural adaptations to the habitats in which they live in order to survive.

The **epidermis** is the outer layer of cells covering the leaf and all parts of the plant. The leaves usually have a waxy coating to make them waterproof. This outer film is called the **cuticle**.

Most plants have green leaves, due to the chlorophyll they contain. Under the top surface of the leaves is a layer of special cells called **palisade cells**. Inside each cell there are tiny disk-shaped containers called **chloroplasts**, which are full of chlorophyll. The chloroplasts can move within the cell to take advantage of exposure to sunlight.

Chlorophyll absorbs blue, red, and violet light energy from the sun, but reflects the green light energy. It is a green pigment that traps energy from sunlight so that it can be used to convert carbon dioxide, from the air, and water, from the ground, into a sugar food.

A leaf has veins that carry water and minerals to the leaf and take away the food made in the leaf. The large main veins in the center, that resemble a spine, are called the midrib. Mid-sized veins branch off from the midrib, and even smaller veinlets branch off the midsize veins. The veins of plants also act as skeletons, making the leaves stronger and giving them their shape.

Leaves have tiny, slitlike openings on them called **stomata**. They are found mostly on the undersides of leaves. Gases and water vapor pass in and out through the stomata. A plant also uses the stomata to control the rate at which it loses water: They can remain closed to prevent water loss. They are usually open during the day to allow gases in for photosynthesis. At night, they are usually closed to prevent water loss.

Another important function in water transport to plant cells is **osmosis**. If one cell contains a weak solution (a little sugar with lots of water) and is next to another plant cell with a strong solution (a lot of sugar with a little water), the water **molecules** will move from the weak to the strong solution by osmosis.

Flowers

Flowering plants are the most **dominant** plant type in the plant kingdom. There are more than 250,000 species. These species include garden flowers, wildflowers, **fruits**, vegetables, trees, shrubs, grasses, and vines. Two groups of plants reproduce by seeds. The most successful are the **angiosperms**, or *covered* seeds. These produce seeds from flowers. The other group of seed-bearing plants is the **gymnosperms**, or naked seeds. These include ferns and conifers.

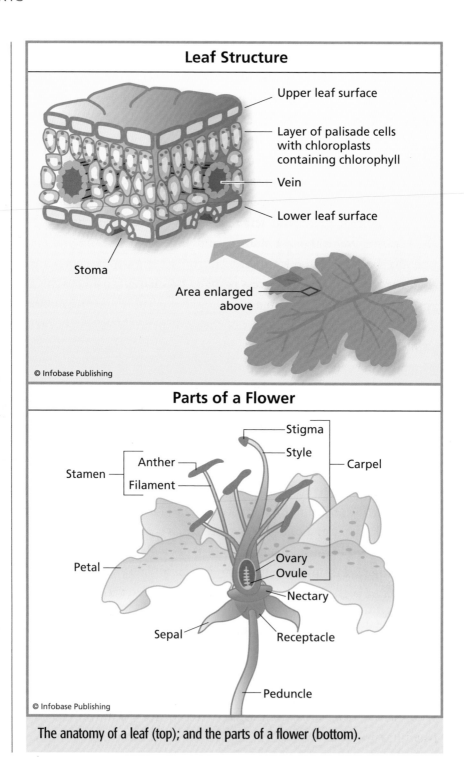

Leaf Structure

Upper leaf surface

Layer of palisade cells with chloroplasts containing chlorophyll

Vein

Lower leaf surface

Stoma

Area enlarged above

© Infobase Publishing

Parts of a Flower

Stigma

Style

Carpel

Stamen

Anther

Filament

Petal

Ovary

Ovule

Nectary

Sepal

Receptacle

Peduncle

© Infobase Publishing

The anatomy of a leaf (top); and the parts of a flower (bottom).

Flowers are the reproductive parts of flowering plants. They produce the seeds that enable the plant to reproduce. Each type of plant has its own special flowers. Some are big, others small; some colorful, others plain; some open during the day, others at night; some are fragrant, others have no smell. But even though flowers vary greatly in appearance, they all have similar basic parts.

The male part is the **stamen**, which produces **pollen**. The female parts are the **pistils**, whose ovaries produce **eggs**. The flowers of some plants have both male and female parts—both stamens and pistils. Other plants may only have stamens, and others only pistils.

In order for seeds to form, there must be a transfer of pollen from a stamen to a pistil. This process is called **pollination**. Pollination can occur when pollen falls from a stamen onto a pistil of the same flower or onto a pistil of another flower of the same plant. Most plants, however, depend on animals or wind to carry pollen from one flower to another of the same plant.

A flower's shape, color, sweet **nectar**, and smell are designed to attract animals to help pollinate it. Birds and insects visit the flower, become covered in pollen dust, move off to another flower, and deposit some of the collected pollen onto the next flower, thereby pollinating that flower.

Most plants cross-pollinate. This means they need pollen from another similar plant to make seeds. They rely on the wind, water, and insects to carry pollen. A flower's shape, structure, color, and smell determine how it is pollinated. Wind-pollinated flowers may be dull and drab-looking because they do not need to attract pollinators. Produced in high quantities, the pollen granules are very light and are carried from plant to plant by air currents. This is the pollen that causes hay fever in humans. Insect-pollinated flowers, on the other hand, are usually very colorful and sweet smelling in order to attract the insects.

Fertilization takes place when a male sex cell fuses with a female sex cell. For this to happen in a flowering plant, the male sex cell has to travel from the pollen grain right down into the **ovary** of the female part of the flower.

Insects pollinate flowers. These are monarch butterflies, which travel from flower to flower. *(Courtesy of U.S. Fish and Wildlife Service; photo by Allen Montgomery)*

Germination

It is critical for a plant to scatter its seeds. The seeds need to move away from the parent plant so that "parent" and "child" do not have to compete with each other for survival over space, light, water, and nutrients.

The number of seeds produced by a plant depends on the amount of rain that it receives, the temperature, and other factors. There are a variety of seed-scattering methods in the plant kingdom. Factors in the natural environment can also affect how far a seed is **dispersed**. Most seeds have some type of dispersal mechanism, or characteristic, which enables the seed to scatter or travel a distance. A seed's dispersal mechanism often reflects the conditions within the habitat. Dispersal mechanisms can also be driven by the seasons.

Plants that live in the water have their seeds carried away by water currents. Floating on water spreads coconuts. Seeds that are scattered by the wind are structurally designed to "fly." For example, dandelions have parachutes, while other plants have "wings." Other plants can physically eject their seeds into the air. Other seeds, such as those in fruit, are eaten by birds and mammals and then later scattered in their droppings. Some seeds, like burs, have tiny hooks that catch in fur or feathers and are transported until they fall off or are pulled off.

Some plants can reproduce without making seeds. Plants, such as strawberries, send out long stems that creep over the ground's surface. At the tip of the stem, a little plantlet develops. It forms shoots and leaves and sends tiny, new roots into the ground to begin a new strawberry plant. This type of **reproduction** is called *cloning*. Although a huge quantity of seeds can be dispersed, only a few will actually successfully grow. The full potential is never reached. Only when soil moisture, temperature, and other conditions are right, will a seed begin to grow into a new plant. This process is called **germination**.

When the seed soaks up water and swells, an **embryo** root is able to break out of the coating that surrounds the seed and, using energy from the food stored in the seed, to grow longer. Then the first shoot pushes upward out of the ground. Once leaves grow from the shoot, the plant begins to produce its own food. **Annual** plants only bloom for one season. **Perennial** plants bloom each year from the same plants (such as tulips).

Growth does not take place evenly throughout a plant. Growth occurs at the tips of roots and stems. In tree trunks and branches, there is a layer called **cambium**, which lies between the xylem and the phloem. The cambium is a growth tissue. As it grows, it forms new xylem (on the inside), and phloem (on the outside). The old xylem becomes wood, and the old phloem becomes bark. The bark acts as a skin to protect the tree from animals, diseases, and keeps the tree from drying out.

DIVERSITY AND UNITY

In the plant world, there is not only diversity *of* species but also diversity *within* species. The variation of **organisms** within a species increases the likelihood that at least some members of the species will survive under changed environmental conditions. Likewise, a great diversity of different species is beneficial because it increases the chance that at least some living things will survive in the face of large changes in the environment—such as extreme climatic changes.

In any ecosystem, species depend on one another and on their environment for survival. Species both cooperate and compete with each other. The interrelationships and interdependencies of organisms work together to generate an environment that can remain stable for hundreds, or thousands, of years. In addition, an organism's ability to regulate its internal environment enables the organism to obtain and use resources, grow, reproduce, and maintain stable, internal conditions while living in a constantly changing external environment.

Plants have a great variety of body designs and internal structures that serve specific functions for survival, such as leaves and stems in photosynthesis and mineral transport in plants. Plants can react to internal and environmental stimuli through behavioral responses. For example, they have tissues and **organs** that react to light, water, and other stimuli.

TROPISMS

Plants can change their growth in response to their environment. These changes are referred to as **tropisms**. There are four basic types of tropism:

Honey Guides

Plants use brightly colored petals to attract insects. Some plants have dark markings on the petals. The markings trace a line toward the center of the flower where the nectar is stored inside. These special markings are referred to as *honey guides* and aid in the pollination of the flower by literally pointing the insect in the proper direction in order to pollinate it.

- *Phototropism:* The way a plant grows or bends in response to light.
- *Geotropism:* The way a plant grows or bends in response to gravity.
- *Hydrotropism:* The way a plant grows or bends in response to water.
- *Thigmotropism:* The way a plant grows or bends in response to touch or physical contact.

Responses can be positive or negative. A positive response is when the plant moves toward, or in the direction of, the **stimulus**. A negative response is when a plant moves away from the stimulus. Roots respond positively to gravity by growing down into the soil.

The trunk and branches respond negatively to gravity by growing up toward the sky. However, the trunk and branches have a positive phototropism, because they grow toward the light.

Tropisms help a plant survive in its environment. When a root responds positively to gravity, it is able to grow toward water and nutrient sources. When leaves on a plant grow toward the direction of sunlight, it helps them survive and produce food. Indoor plants left sitting on a windowsill demonstrate this tropism. Because the leaves

Growing Your Own Plant From Germplasm

Germplasm is a term used to describe the genetic resources, or more precisely the DNA, of an organism and collections of that material. They are seeds, **cuttings**, or whole plants. Remove a stem from a plant with three or four leaves. If you place the stem in a glass of water and put it in a light area (just not direct sunlight), within a few days, tiny roots will begin to appear from the cut stem. After a couple of weeks, there will be a small network of roots. At this point, the stem can be planted in soil. By keeping it in a light place with plenty of moisture, it will soon grow into a plant.

An example of geotropism. The tree, growing on a hillside, rights itself under the influence of gravity. *(Photo by Julie A. Kerr, Nature's Images)*

An example of thigmotropism. These trees are permanently bent in the direction of the persistent wind pattern in Texas. *(Photo by Larry Howell)*

grow toward the source of light, if the plant is turned 180 degrees, the leaves will reorient themselves back again to the source of light. There are many unique tropisms in rain forests in order to ensure a plant's survival. Because vegetation lives at different canopy levels, it has had to adapt in order to reach sunlight and nutrients. Leaves are usually large and maximize sun exposure, especially in the lower canopy levels where the sunlight is not as intense. Other plants, like vines, may have to climb up the trunks of other trees in order to reach sufficient light in order to manufacture food through the process of photosynthesis.

PLANT ADAPTATIONS—MECHANISMS OF SURVIVAL

Each kind of plant has adaptations that allow it to live in a specific environment. From orchids in Hawaii and coconut trees in the warm tropics to pine trees in cold mountain climates, or from wildflowers in moist meadows, to cactus in desolate, hot desert regions—all plants have adapted in some way to their environment. If they had not, they could not survive there.

Several factors determine what types of plants can successfully grow there. For example, temperature, rainfall, amount of sunlight, wind, soil type, the interaction of other plants as well as animals, and the effects of urbanization all play a critical role in determining which types of plants will be successful.

In desert regions, typical flowers do not grow there because it is not only too hot, but there is very little rainfall. Some areas may not receive any rain for months, or even years. But when rainfall does occur, a seemingly colorless, empty desert can suddenly bloom profusely as carpets of tiny plants appear in response to the rain. These plants grow quickly, producing flowers, which then produce a new crop of seeds. The entire life cycle—from seed to flower to seed—may be completed in just 10 days. The seeds can then lie dormant in the ground for years, awaiting the next significant rainfall event. For a few short days, the desert can be filled with beautiful, colored flowers.

Cacti have also adapted to regions of infrequent rainfall. They produce their food and store water in their thick stems rather than in leaves. The thin spines on their stems help prevent water loss. Cacti have also adapted in other ways to their hostile environment. Cacti grow many long roots, which grow close to the surface and spread in all directions so that water can be soaked up quickly after light rainfalls. The water gets stored in the stem and is used during periods of drought. The saguaro cactus can store enough water in its stem to last about three years. On the other hand, plants in the tropical rain forests have huge, wide leaves with many stomata so that they can quickly eliminate excess water.

Because trees cannot grow when temperatures fall below freezing, they shed their leaves to protect against losing water. During the winter, trees do not carry out photosynthesis. During this **dormant period,** they depend on their stored food to stay alive.

Cacti have adapted to their harsh desert environment. They have thorns not only for protection, but also to reduce and prevent water loss. *(Photo by Jerel G. Casper, Nature's Images)*

In extremely cold areas, such as the slopes of high mountains or the Arctic or Antarctic, plants must find ways to survive the cold temperatures and harsh winds. Some of the plants in these regions develop hairy leaves to trap warmth from the sun and keep from drying out in the wind. An alpine plant called the alpine snowbell, actually warms the area immediately around it to melt a tiny area of snow so that it can grow in the frozen ground. Many high mountain plants grow close to the ground in thick clumps to keep warm and out of the wind. In hot, dry desert areas, plants will have needles instead of leaves to help them retain water and keep predators away.

Plants can adapt in their environment to protect and defend themselves against insects, animals, people, and even other plants. Some plants have developed special roots or hairs to get the water they need.

Some plants are **parasites**—they have huge sucking roots—and get their food and water from other plants.

Other plants have thorns, prickers, or poison in order to protect themselves. The thorns of a rosebush are an example of this type of defense. Another is the stinging nettle, which grows in fields among grasses and weeds and is covered with dozens of tiny hollow hairs. At the base of each hair is a container filled with poison. When an animal, or person, brushes against the stinging nettle, the tips of the hairs break off. The hairs enter the skin, introducing poison into the victim.

There are also carnivorous (meat-eating) plants that have special leaves to trap insects. There are several types of carnivorous plants. A common one is the Venus fly trap. The leaves on this plant contain tiny, sensitive hairs. If an insect lands on the plant and trips the hairs, the plant's two hinged sides close shut like a clam, trapping the insect within.

The sundew is another meat eater. The hairs on the sundew's leaves produce a sticky, digestive liquid that looks like droplets of water. When an insect lands for a drink, it gets stuck in the liquid drops and cannot escape. The special liquid then digests them.

Devil's Claw

The devil's claw is a plant that spreads its seeds in a way similar to burrs—via animals. The devil's claw, however, is several inches in size. It has two horns, or claws, attached to it. The seed capsule usually contains about 40 seeds, which are gradually released when the claws split apart. In some areas of the southwestern United States, they are a nuisance to sheep ranchers because they can easily become entangled in a sheep's fleece. The seed capsules are also adapted for hitchhiking on the hooves of large grazing animals. In some areas, American Indians know the huge seeds as *ihug* (EE-hook). These seed capsules can have claws up to 15 inches (38 cm) long. They are often used in basket making.

One of the oddest carnivorous plants is the pitcher plant. It is built like a narrow, deep vase. On the outside, it contains a "false flower"—it looks like a beautiful flower, but it is really a large leaf tip. The sweet-smelling nectar attracts the insect to the lid, but in order to reach the nectar, the insect must climb down into the flower. The mouth and walls of the inside are extremely slippery. As the insect slips and falls into the pitcher, special downward-pointing hairs keep it from being able to climb back up. The insect falls to the bottom inside the pitcher and drowns in the digestive juices. The plant absorbs the minerals from the insect. Only the shell of the insect's body is left to collect in the bottom of the plant.

Another survival strategy is found in the passionflower, which has odd leaves. The leaves have strange growths on them that resemble butterfly eggs. This "camouflage" keeps butterflies from laying real eggs on the leaves. The "false eggs" protect the plant from the caterpillars that would have hatched from real butterfly eggs and eaten the leaves.

Nature's Velcro

Velcro—the popular fastener used on shoes, clothes, backpacks, and hundreds of other items—was actually invented based on the behavior of the cocklebur. One day, in 1948, a Swiss mountaineer, George de Mestral, took his dog on a walk through a field of bur plants. When he and his dog returned home, they were covered with cockle burs. Curious, Mestral put one under his microscope and examined it. He saw dozens of small hooks that enabled the seed-bearing bur to stick to the tiny loops in the fabric of his pants.

Realizing the potential of what he was looking at, Mestral decided to design a unique, two-sided fastener: one side with stiff hooks like the cockle burs, and the other side with soft loops like the fabric of pants. He called his new invention Velcro—which was a combination of the words *velour* and *crochet*—and the rest is history.

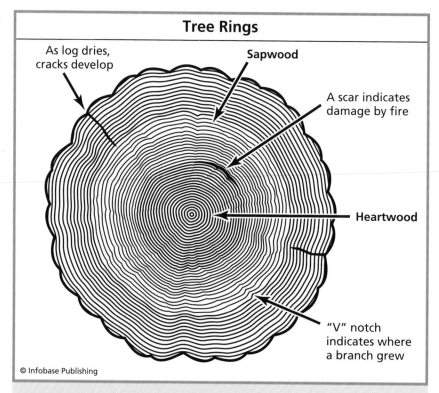

Tree Rings

As log dries, cracks develop

Sapwood

A scar indicates damage by fire

Heartwood

"V" notch indicates where a branch grew

© Infobase Publishing

The study of tree rings can help climatologists identify years of drought and other natural occurrences.

Stone plants in South Africa are camouflaged to look just like the rocks that surround them. This keeps hungry animals from eating them.

YEARLY CYCLES

Deciduous trees, such as oak and aspen, change their appearance with the seasons. At the beginning of spring, branches are bare. By summer, the tree has grown a new set of leaves, and flowers have appeared. After pollination, seeds and fruits develop. Then, with the onset of autumn and cooler temperatures, the leaves change color and fall off the tree. The fruits that have grown during the summer begin to be dispersed or are eaten by animals (such as birds and squirrels). During the winter, the tree is nearly dormant. They may have buds on the branches, but they do not open until spring when the temperatures are warmer.

Many trees can live several hundred years, repeating this growth pattern with the endless cycle of seasons. Each year, a tree grows bigger. Its trunk and branches grow longer and thicker in order to support the tree's extra weight from growth. The roots spread farther underground to anchor the tree and take in more water and nutrients.

The trunk and branches grow fatter because a new layer of wood grows each year under the bark. This new layer is called **sapwood**. Sapwood is soft, living wood that carries food and water through the tree. The older wood in the center is called **heartwood**, which is hard and dead. Its job is to support the trunk, like a steel beam supports a building. Most of the wood in a tree trunk is dead heartwood.

A tree's new layer of sapwood grows in a ring shape around the heartwood. A new distinct ring grows each year. This allows the age of a tree to be measured—each ring represents one year's growth. They are referred to as annual rings.

Climatologists can study tree rings and determine what the climate was like during the different stages of growth. Wide rings indicate a good growing season with plenty of rain. Narrow rings are a result of dry years.

THE EVOLUTION AND ADAPTATION OF PLANTS

The plant kingdom is as diverse in type and behavior as the animal kingdom. The smallest plants—such as some green algae—are smaller than the smallest animals. The largest known plants—such as redwoods and the giant sequoia—are as big as blue whales in size.

Plants grow in diverse habitats and on every continent. In order to survive in a wide range of habitats and environments, plants have developed many different mechanisms. Some plants complete their life cycle in less than a month. Others, such as palm trees and cacti take many years to reach maturity. This chapter examines how plants have evolved over time in order to adapt to their surroundings. It looks at what extinction really is, how plant species are classified, and what species are **endangered**.

ADAPTATIONS AND SURVIVAL

At Earth's beginning, living things could not survive on Earth because the atmosphere contained poisonous gases, and the heat from the sunlight was too strong. The first plants lived in the nutrient-rich ocean more than 3 billion years ago.

Scientists believe these plants were one-celled organisms that probably developed from simple bacteria and were similar to algae and contained chlorophyll with which to produce their own food. Blue-green algae, called *cyanobacteria*, are some of the oldest life-forms and still survive in watery environments today. They are found in environments as extreme as Arctic pack ice and boiling hot springs.

Certain conditions had to be overcome before plants could live on land. For example, they needed to develop a watertight skin to keep them from drying out. They also needed to develop stems in order to support the plant upright out of the water as well as provide a means to obtain water from the ground. They had to develop a way to reproduce without relying on the ocean.

Primitive plants needed a damp environment so that plants could reproduce sexually by having male and female cells come together. Primitive plants like mosses still reproduce this way.

About 400 million years ago, plants began to develop that were better able to invade the land while not needing to live in the water. Scientists believe the first land plants were probably sea plants that were stranded when the tide went out or when the pool of water they lived in dried up. The plants then adapted to life on land.

The very first land plants were extremely simple—they had stems but no leaves. These primitive land plants did not have a water-transport system, so they grew near lakes. They were the ancestors of the **spore**-bearing plants, such as mosses and ferns. Plants then adapted by growing roots in order to take in water from the ground and growing green leaves to make food.

At first, plants grew close to the ground. But as more types developed, they had to compete for space and sunlight, so they adapted and grew taller.

When plants photosynthesize, they give off oxygen as a waste product. These early plants played a crucial role in the adaptations and survival of other organisms. The air was originally thick with poisonous gases, such as methane and ammonia, but no oxygen. Gradually, the plants put enough oxygen into the air for animals to develop and survive. Plants in the water also played a significant role by putting oxygen into the water. Even today, the oxygen that plants put into the water dissolves and is then "breathed" by fish and other creatures in the ocean.

The primitive plants that developed thick, woody stems became the first trees. Then, giant horsetails, club mosses, and ferns formed in huge swamps. Some horsetails grew as high as 150 feet (46 m).

This point in geologic time was the Carboniferous period (362–290 million years ago). Seed-bearing plants—such as conifers—appeared about 350 million years ago. Flowering plants appeared later—about 135 million years ago. Today, flowering plants are the most common type of plant. These plants contributed to the dinosaur's survival by providing food and oxygen supplies. Unlike the dinosaurs, however, these plants did not become extinct.

During the Carboniferous period, as the trees growing in the swamps died, they sank to the bottom of the swamps. Through millions of years, more and more tree ferns and other green plants fell and compacted the plant (organic) matter beneath it. Earth's climate then experienced many changes, causing the swamps to dry up and the tree ferns to die. The thick layers of dead tree ferns were eventually turned into thick beds of coal, which is the source of the coal that is mined and burned today.

The Mesozoic era, which existed about 250 million to 65 million years ago, is divided into three periods: the Triassic, Jurassic, and Cretaceous. The plants and animals on Earth differed during each of these three periods. The changes in plant life during this era affected the development of animal life. Some scientists believe that the appearance of flowering plants is significant with respect to the extinction of the dinosaurs. Some believe the flowering plants may have poisoned them.

At the end of the Jurassic and beginning of the Cretaceous period, the climate grew drier, the wetlands dried up, and new kinds of trees took over. Plants evolved that relied less and less on water to reproduce. The

Geologic Time Scale

Geologic period	Approximate years	Climate	Predominant life-forms
Precambrian	4,600–570 million years ago	Wet	First one-celled and multi-celled organisms
Cambrian	570–505 million years ago	Wet	First shells, trilobites dominant
Ordovician	505–438 million years ago	Wet	First fish
Silurian	438–408 million years ago	Swampy	First land plant fossils
Devonian	408–362 million years ago	Swampy	First amphibians
Carboniferous	362–290 million years ago	Swampy	Giant horsetails, ferns, club mosses, large primitive trees, giant amphibians, and dragonflies
Permian	290–245 million years ago	Cooler	Conifers, ginkgoes, and other primitive plants
Triassic	245–208 million years ago	Drier	Cycads and meat-eating dinosaurs
Jurassic	208–145 million years ago	Cooler and wetter	Swamp cypress, ferns, longneck dinosaurs, and flying reptiles
Cretaceous	145–65 million years ago	Drier	Horned dinosaurs, snakes, and flowering plants, bulrushes, and willow trees
Tertiary	65–2 million years ago	Drier	Earliest large mammals; extinction of dinosaurs (at the Cretaceous-Tertiary boundary 65 million years ago)
Quaternary	0–2 million years ago	Drier	Appearance of humans

new types of plants grew from seeds and relied on the wind to transport the male cells to the female ones. The first flowering plants—the angiosperms—developed that were able to utilize other ways to reproduce.

Scientists have been able to reconstruct the history of plants through the study of **fossil** records. The oldest land plants to be preserved as fossils date back to about 400 million years ago and had already developed water-carrying tissues—the xylem and phloem—which allowed them to stand upright.

Dispersal or Drift?

Over 250 million years ago, all the continents of Earth formed a single land mass called Pangaea. Then, about 50 million years later, this supercontinent began to split in two. One piece, called Laurasia, is now North America, Asia, and Europe. The other piece, called Gondwana, is now present-day Antarctica, Australia, South America, Africa, and India. About 80 million years ago, New Zealand split off of Gondwana. Then, about 35 million years ago, South America and Australia separated from Antarctica. The breaking up of the continents is called continental drift.

Today, plant life on New Zealand shares striking similarities to that on other Southern Hemisphere landmasses. For example, one genus, *Nothofagus*, a southern beech tree, whose 80-million-year-old fossil history goes back to the days of Gondwana, has many botanists debating how the plant ended up in places separated by such vast expanses of ocean.

One theory is that continental drift is responsible for the geological and fossil record similarities and that plant biodiversity is similar because the plants existed on both landmasses when they were hooked together. Then later, when the continents broke apart, each landmass carried the plants with it. Another theory is that the plants' seeds traveled across the ocean in long-range oceanic dispersal. This issue continues to be debated today by botanists.

EXTINCTION—FOREVER LOST

If organisms are to survive, they must be able to adapt to the external, or environmental, conditions. Those that are able to successfully change and adapt to changing external conditions are said to evolve. Those that do not successfully change die out.

By the beginning of the Paleocene epoch (in the Tertiary period), 65 million years ago, the environment changed from its previous state. Flowering plants were able to adapt and dominate the plant kingdom. At the same time, the dinosaurs were not able to adapt and became extinct.

An explosion of insect diversity seemed to correlate with the abundance of flowering plants, which enabled flowering plants to survive because the insects could pollinate them. Species depend on one another and on the environment for their survival. It is these delicate interrelationships and interdependencies among organisms that generate stable ecosystems. It allows an ecosystem to remain in a state of rough equilibrium for a long period of time.

As external conditions change, organisms must adapt to those changes if they are going to survive. Abiotic (nonliving) factors, such as climate, can have a major impact on the adaptation and evolution of organisms. That is one reason why, today, the impact humans have on the environment is so important. If human activity alters an area more, or faster, than organisms can adapt, they will be unable to survive and will become extinct.

When the environment changes, the adaptive characteristics of some species are insufficient to allow for their survival. Extinction is common in the life-forms throughout Earth's history. In fact, most of the species that have lived on Earth no longer exist.

The process of natural selection leads to organisms that are well-suited for survival in particular environments. Therefore, when an environment changes, some inherited characteristics become more or less advantageous or neutral, and chance alone can result in characteristics having no survival or reproductive value.

Natural selection and its evolutionary consequences provide an explanation for the diversity and unity of past and present life-forms on

Earth. This can be seen in recurring patterns of relationships in Earth's fossil record—the millions of different species living today appear to be descendents of common ancestors. The basic concept of adaptivity and evolution is that Earth's present-day life-forms have evolved from earlier, distinctly different species as a result of the interactions of (1) the genetic variability of offspring due to mutation and recombination of genes; (2) the potential for a species to increase its numbers; (3) a finite supply of the resources required for life; and (4) the ensuing selection by the environment of those offspring better suited to survive and leave offspring of their own.

As plants evolved, the composition of Earth's atmosphere also changed. Over time, the poisonous gases were replaced by oxygen. As scientists study fossils, they are able to put the puzzle pieces of geologic time together and determine how life and environmental conditions have changed on Earth over time.

By studying these fossils and plant remains, scientists have a much better understanding of what Earth's environment was like eons ago. They are able to determine that conditions like rising temperatures, changing rainfall patterns, and the melting of glaciers have caused many significant changes to the ecosystems on Earth, resulting in the extinction over time of certain life-forms.

Plants today are still evolving and adapting. The evolution of plants never stops—it is a continuous process.

PLANT SUCCESSION

If land is cleared of its native plant life, new plants will begin to grow in the area. Over the years, different types of plants will replace each other. This transitioning of species over time is called plant **succession**. The regrowth depends on the amount of water and light available to the area and also the fertility of the soil.

Succession takes place where bare land is exposed. This can be anywhere the vegetation has been significantly disturbed: a sand dune, a building lot, a field, grazing pastures, wetlands, or on a mountainside after a severe forest fire or volcanic eruption.

An extreme example is the conversion of a sandy area to a forest. Sand does not hold much organic material, so it is very difficult for plants to thrive on it. Besides the lack of nutrients, sand does not hold water well. Once water enters sand, it percolates down into the ground and is lost. Sand is also easily eroded by wind and water, making it an unstable surface for anything to grow on.

There are grass types, however, that are able to grow in sandy areas. If one of these grasses begins to grow, it sends out many roots. This thick web of roots helps to stabilize the soil and keep it from eroding. When the grass dies, it decays into organic matter and its nutrients become incorporated into the soil. This addition of organic matter enables the soil to begin holding more water.

The environmental conditions have now changed. The soil has become more fertile, inviting other species in. Annual plants may begin to grow. Annuals only live for one year, but they produce a multitude of seeds. This encourages more of the annuals to germinate and grow, which in turn increases the fertility, water-holding ability, and stability of the soil.

Eventually, perennial plants—those that live more than a year—will start to grow. These include shrubs and trees. As trees begin to grow, they shade the ground, which keeps the annuals from being able to survive there. Over time, the area has been transformed from a barren, sandy one to a forest.

Succession also happens with intense cattle grazing. If cattle are allowed to overgraze and destroy the native grasses that grow in the area, leaving the ground bare, an invader species called cheat grass can take over an area and outcompete the native grass. The invader species may disturb the natural balance of an area, making it impossible for the native vegetation to compete and survive. In addition, the new species may not even be edible as a grazing staple. That is one reason why ranchers have to take great care in not letting their herds overgraze the land. Upsetting this delicate balance has been a significant problem in the western United States for many years. This often occurs in the Southwest, where dry conditions persist and drought is common. Once a delicate balance is upset, it is very difficult to reverse it through reclamation efforts.

CLASSIFICATION OF SPECIES

Because there are nearly 400,000 different species of plants, botanists (scientists who study plants) classify them into groups according to their structure. All the species in a group share certain characteristics that make them different from species in other groups. Over the years, various plant classification systems have been developed.

Classifying plants provides a logical system by which they can be accurately identified. Plants are grouped in categories of increasing size. This type of system is called a *hierarchical classification system*. A *systematic classification* takes into account the relationships that exist between plants. The entire classification process is referred to as *taxonomy*.

Hierarchical Classification System

Kingdom

Division (Phylum)

Subdivision (Subphylum)

Class

Subclass

Order

Family

Subfamily

Genus

Subgenus

Species

It was Swedish naturalist Carolus Linnaeus (1707–1778) who established, in 1753, the system of binomial nomenclature for plants. His published work was called *Species Plantarum*.

Today, The International Code of Botanical Nomenclature (ICBN) controls the naming of plants into an accepted hierarchical system of classification. This system identifies principal ranks of diminishing size.

Any system of classification relies on the accumulation of vast amounts of data about plants. The classification takes into consideration its basic plant parts (called morphology), flowers, and reproductive organs. Plants are also analyzed under microscopes. A plant's breeding system, chemical composition, chromosomes, **ecology**, and geographical distribution are all studied.

Major Groups of Plants

Major group	Common members	Specific characteristics
Pteridophyta "Wing plants"	Ferns	Vascular plants; have leaves called fronds; reproduce by spores that form on the undersides of leaves
Bryophyta "Mosses"	Mosses, liverworts, hornworts	Nonvascular; small plants; reproduce by spores; live in wet places
Coniferophyta "Cone-bearing plants"	Conifers (i.e., spruce, cedar, pine, sequoia, firs)	Vascular trees; needlelike leaves; usually reproduce by seeds in pinecones
Magnoliophya "Flowering plants"	Flowering plants	Vascular plants; seeds are enclosed in fruit that forms from the ovary of the flower

The basic unit of plant classification is the species. A species is a group of individual plants that have characteristics in common and usually breed with each other to produce similar offspring.

All classification schemes refer to species by a double name, or binomial, which is internationally accepted. The binomial is always in Latin and is given only after a detailed investigation into the plant's relationships to other similar plants and its place in the scheme.

To be strictly scientific, the name of a plant should consist of three distinct parts. The first is the generic name, which refers to the genus; the second is the specific epithet, which identifies the different species within the genus (genus and species form the binomial). The third part is the name of the botanical author who first correctly described the species.

Taxonomy is based on the construction of data matrices (tables) between species, genera, and on up. Botanists use computers to store and analyze the information. Plants are grouped based on their similarities to other plants.

This is one way scientists can monitor plants and their environmental conditions. This enables scientists to keep an active inventory and become alerted if a plant faces being endangered (threatened with extinction).

ENDANGERED SPECIES AND TRENDS

Because the impact of human activity on the land can threaten or endanger plant species, scientists have become more aware of impacts, and environmentalists have taken action to stop the negative impacts of human activity on plant ecosystems in order to prevent extinction.

In 1973, the U.S. government passed the Endangered Species Act in order to provide a practical means to monitor and conserve the ecosystems on which endangered and threatened species depend and to provide programs for the conservation of those species, in order to prevent their extinction. The Interior Department's Fish and Wildlife Service and the United States Commerce Department's National

Oceanic and Atmospheric Administration (NOAA) Fisheries Service administer the law.

This legislation is important in order to preserve and conserve our botanical resources. Since the law was enacted, there has still been a steady increase of endangered and threatened species. For example, in 1980, 59 plant species were listed as threatened or endangered. By 1985, 118 species were listed; by 1990, 240 species; by 1995, 525 species; and by 2000, 736 species. Today, 599 plant species are listed as endangered in the United States, and 147 species are listed as threatened, for a total of 746 plant species.

As populations continue to grow and more pressure is put on the land, these issues become critical. In Chapter 8, which covers conservation, this issue will be looked at in greater depth.

3

RENEWABLE AND NONRENEWABLE RESOURCES

There are two general classes of resources: renewable and non-renewable. This chapter focuses on the various plant resources, the important physical cycles that affect them, their relationships with the environment, and the short- and long-term effects of natural and human-caused environmental change.

TYPES OF BOTANICAL RESOURCES
AND THE IMPORTANCE OF RENEWABILITY

A renewable resource is a resource that can be replenished. It is a resource that can be replaced through natural ecological cycles or good management practices. The opposite of this is a nonrenewable resource—a resource that cannot be replenished (once it is gone, it is gone for good). For practical applications, some scientists consider a renewable resource one that can be replenished within one generation of a human's lifetime (approximately 20–30 years).

For many classes of resources, it is easy to determine which are renewable and which are not. For example, with energy resources, **fossil fuels** (oil and petroleum) and coal are not renewable because they took millions of years to form. Even though the same geological processes are still happening today, these resources will not be replaced within our lifetime. Energy resources, such as wind power and water-power, are considered renewable because they are readily abundant and can be generated within a short time period.

Botanical resources involve ecosystems, which are fragile and complex. All elements of living systems are interwoven; in other words, if one element is affected, the entire system is affected. Compare these interactions to a car: a car will work well as long as all the individual components are being taken care of and functioning right; but, if suddenly one of the parts is neglected or damaged and stops working properly—like the engine running out of oil—it impacts the entire system. If one component stops working the way it should, the entire system is jeopardized, and until that one component is managed correctly and repaired, the system fails or is unproductive.

Plants are a highly valuable resource. They are the basis of healthy ecosystems and perform important functions, such as purifying the air and water. Humans, and other life-forms, depend on the oxygen that is given off as a by-product from photosynthesis in plants. Plants are also important in the water cycle—more than 90% of the water that is taken in through a plant's roots is eventually released back to the atmosphere in a process called transpiration.

Plants provide the basis of most food webs on Earth. They provide protection and shelter by providing wood to construct homes and cotton to make clothing. In addition, plants provide shelter and habitat for many other animals as well. For example, a single tree in the rain forest can be a home to more than 1,000 different insect species.

Plants are also used in medicines. From traditional herbal remedies to components of prescription drugs, plants play a vital role each day in our health and well-being. Plants provide energy to make our lives more convenient. Coal was formed from decayed vegetation millions of years ago. In addition to this source of energy, technology exists today to produce biofuels from corn and other biomass. As technology improves, ethanol—the fuel produced from corn—may someday replace the fossil fuels the world currently relies on so heavily.

Many industrial products are made from plants. For example, plants provide the ingredients for commodities such as soap, glue, pencil erasers, bath powder, cosmetics, body lotions, nail polish remover, plastics, and high-quality industrial lubricants.

Plants also have an intangible value. Although it cannot be specifically measured, plants do provide an important aesthetic value to life. Whether used as landscaping, ornamental decorations, flower arrangements, or in many other forms, plants play an important role in our pleasure as well as cultural traditions. For example, what would Christmas be without evergreen trees—or weddings without flowers?

Plants provide some of the most critical food staples. The most common and important plants in the world are grasses. Not only do they provide food for most domesticated and wild animals, they supply much of the world's sugar in the form of sugarcane. All the cereal crops, such as corn, wheat, oats, rye, barley, rice, and millet are grasses.

Although it may seem that plants are renewable, that may not be the case. For example, if an aggressive plant or weed infests an area, it can crowd out native (natural) plants by monopolizing vital nutrients in the soil so that the native plants cannot survive. If the invasive plant takes over, the native plant has become nonrenewable in that area as long as those conditions persist.

A plant's availability and productivity are both part of a complex system that must remain delicately balanced in order to function. The key to understanding this balance lies in understanding the important natural cycles that determine a plant's success.

THE IMPORTANT RESOURCE CYCLES: MAINTAINING A DELICATE BALANCE

The cycles that are critical to a plant's survival and growth are the water, carbon, nitrogen, oxygen, and soil cycles.

The Water Cycle

Water is necessary for plant growth, for dissolving and transporting plant nutrients, and for the survival of soil organisms. The water cycle is fundamental to all life on Earth. From rainfall to a fast-moving stream to the movement of water through the ground, water is always in motion. The endless movement and recycling of water between the atmosphere, the land's surface, and underground is called the water cycle, or the hydrologic cycle.

Two separate forces make the water cycle work: the energy of the sun and the force of Earth's gravity. Water vapor is carried through the atmosphere by air currents. When the air cools, it condenses, forming clouds. Some of the moisture falls back to Earth as rain, snow, hail, or sleet.

Once the water reaches the ground, it can go in several directions before it returns again to the atmosphere. Plants can use the water, which can also be stored in lakes, or can seep into the soil. The sun's energy can then make the water evaporate back into the atmosphere, or Earth's gravity can pull the water that has entered the ground down through the soil to be stored for years as slowly moving groundwater.

Groundwater can be stored in aquifers (natural underground reservoirs), or it can eventually seep into springs and resurface. Water on the surface is returned to the atmosphere through the process of **evaporation**. Water that has been used by plants is returned to the atmosphere as vapor through transpiration, which happens when water passes through the leaves of plants. These two functions together are called *evapotranspiration*. Evapotranspiration is greatest in areas that are hot, dry, sunny, or windy.

Although water is critical for plant growth and transporting nutrients, it can also be a destructive force if not managed properly. It can cause soil compaction, which clumps the particles of soil close together and removes the important air space needed for nutrients to move through the soil; it can leach (remove) nutrients from the soil; and too much water can cause excess runoff and **erosion**.

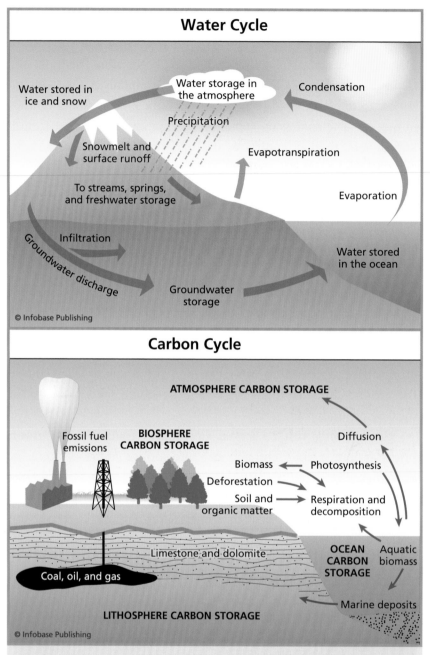

Water Cycle

Water stored in
ice and snow

Water storage in
the atmosphere

Condensation

Precipitation

Snowmelt and
surface runoff

Evapotranspiration

To streams, springs,
and freshwater storage

Evaporation

Infiltration

Groundwater discharge

Water stored
in the ocean

Groundwater
storage

© Infobase Publishing

Carbon Cycle

ATMOSPHERE CARBON STORAGE

Fossil fuel
emissions

**BIOSPHERE
CARBON STORAGE**

Diffusion

Biomass ← Photosynthesis

Deforestation →

Soil and → Respiration and
organic matter   decomposition

Limestone and dolomite

**OCEAN
CARBON
STORAGE**

Aquatic
biomass

Coal, oil, and gas

Marine deposits

LITHOSPHERE CARBON STORAGE

© Infobase Publishing

The crucial resource cycles that determine which plants thrive in an ecosystem:
(top) the water cycle; (bottom) the carbon cycle; and (opposite top) the nitrogen cycle.

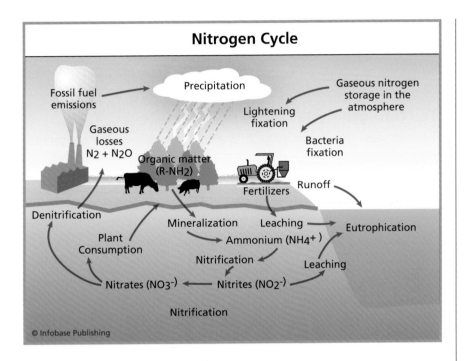

Nitrogen Cycle

The Carbon Cycle

The carbon cycle is important because carbon is the basic structural material for all cell life. Carbon makes the soil productive, and plants healthy. The carbon cycle occurs with movement of carbon between the atmosphere, the oceans, the land, and living organisms.

The atmosphere and plants exchange carbon. Plants absorb carbon dioxide from the atmosphere during photosynthesis and then release carbon dioxide back into the atmosphere during respiration.

Another major exchange of carbon dioxide happens between the oceans and the atmosphere. Ocean plants use the dissolved carbon dioxide in the oceans during photosynthesis.

Carbon is also exchanged through the soil. Plant and animal residues decompose and form organic matter, which contains carbon. For plants to be able to use these nutrients, soil organisms break them down in a process called mineralization.

Animals give off carbon dioxide when they breathe. Some plants are eaten by grazing animals, which then return organic carbon to the soil as manure. Easily broken-down forms of carbon in manure and plant cells are released as carbon dioxide. Forms of carbon that are difficult to break down become stabilized in the soil as humus.

The Nitrogen Cycle

The nitrogen cycle is the process by which nitrogen in the atmosphere enters the soil and becomes part of living organisms before returning to the atmosphere. Nitrogen makes up 78% of Earth's atmosphere. But this nitrogen must be converted from a gas into a chemically usable form before living organisms can use it. This transformation takes place through the nitrogen cycle. It transforms the nitrogen gas into ammonia or nitrates.

Most of the nitrogen conversion process is done biologically. This is done by free-living, nitrogen-fixing bacteria; bacteria living on the roots of plants; and through certain algae and lichens.

Nitrogen that has been converted to ammonia and nitrates is used directly by plants and is absorbed in their tissues as plant **protein**. The nitrogen then passes from plants to **herbivores** (plant-eating animals) and then to **carnivores** (meat-eating animals).

When plants and animals die, decomposition into ammonia breaks down the nitrogen compounds. Plants then use some of this ammonia, and the rest is either dissolved or held in the soil. If it is dissolved or held in the soil, microorganisms then go to work on it in a process called nitrification. Nitrates can be stored in humus or washed from the soil and carried away to streams and lakes. Nitrates may also be converted and returned to the atmosphere by a process called denitrification.

The nitrogen cycle is important because plants need nitrogen to grow, develop, and produce seeds. The main source of nitrogen in soil is from organic matter (humus). Bacteria that live in the soil convert organic forms of nitrogen to inorganic forms that plants can use. Plant roots then take up nitrogen. When the plant dies, it decays and becomes part of the organic matter in the soil. The land must be well managed, or nitrogen can be washed out of the soil, which then negatively impacts the growth of plants.

The Oxygen Cycle

The oxygen cycle follows the same paths as the carbon cycle because oxygen is part of carbon dioxide. Oxygen is also present in water. It is released to the atmosphere during plant photosynthesis.

The carbon/oxygen cycle involves three major processes and one minor process: photosynthesis, respiration, combustion, and decomposition. During photosynthesis, green plants and trees take in carbon dioxide and water using the chlorophyll in their leaves and energy from the sun. They release oxygen, sugar, and water vapor.

Soil Resources

The health of soil resources is related to factors such as fertility, fragility, and erosion. Land use and land management have a tremendous impact on the health of the soil.

Because soil is a nonrenewable resource (i.e., it takes longer than a generation to form), protecting soil quality is very important. Soil is critical in many ways: it provides homes to organisms, decomposes wastes, filters contaminants from water, is used to grow plants, and plays a role in gas exchange (which keeps the resource cycles going). Because there is a limited amount of soil, it must be properly cared for.

The type of soil and what actually goes on in the soil determine how well plants grow. Five factors determine what types of soil form on Earth: (1) parent material, (2) organisms, (3) topography, (4) climate, and (5) time.

Parent material is the primary material from which the soil is formed. Soil parent material can be bedrock; organic material; deposits from water, wind, glaciers, and volcanoes; or an old soil surface. Bedrock is broken down as weathering processes wear away the mineral particles from rocks.

Organisms that live in the soil, along with decaying organic matter from leaves and dead plants, change the soil's chemistry. The most fertile soils have healthy amounts of nitrogen (N), phosphorus (P), and potassium (K). In order to grow healthy and strong, plants need these three elements.

Topography, or how steep or flat the land is, also affects soil due to climatic processes. Soils at the bottoms of hills get more water than soils on slopes. Soils on slopes that face the sun are drier than soils on slopes that do not face the sun. Topography also affects mineral accumulations, types of vegetation, plant nutrients, erosion, and the location of streams—which in turn affect soil formation.

Climate plays an important role. Heating, cooling, wetting, and drying all help break down the parent material that forms the soil. Climate also determines how fast this breakdown occurs.

Time is a critical factor. The longer the natural soil-forming processes occur, the more soil is formed.

Soil protects plant roots from exposure to the sun's heat. It also filters pollution that comes from rain and water runoff from farms. Plants utilize soil to grow and receive support while they grow.

THE FOOD WEB—FEEDING EVERYONE

Energy flows through an ecosystem just as water, carbon, and nitrogen do. Energy is transferred through a **community** as organisms produce and consume food.

Energy flows from producers to consumers as each population eats and is eaten. A **food chain** is a series of organisms that feeds on other organisms. For example, if grass is at the beginning of the chain, it may then be eaten by a grasshopper. The chain continues as a mouse eats the grasshopper, a snake eats the mouse, and finally, an eagle eats the snake. In this example, grass is at the bottom of the food chain, and the eagle is at the top.

Green plants are the *primary producers* because they trap the energy from the sun and use it first. Energy passes from the plants to all other life. Plants (producers) are eaten by herbivores (vegetable-eating animals such as caterpillars and cattle). These are the *primary consumers*. The animals that eat the herbivores are called *secondary consumers* and are meat eaters, or carnivores. Higher consumers, in turn, may eat the carnivores.

Both plants and animals use up their energy for movement and growth, with a lot being lost through respiration. This means that the

Food Webs

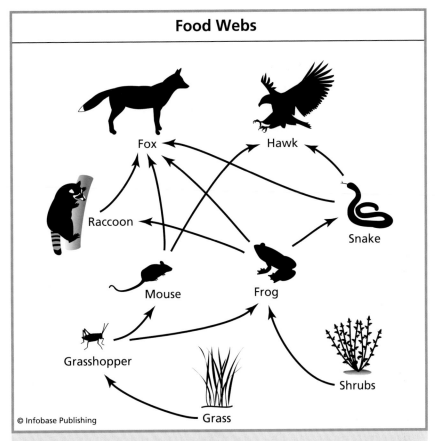

A food web typical of North America. A food web can be very complex, consisting of many interwoven food chains. If one species in the food web is eliminated, it affects the health of the entire food web, illustrating the interdependence of all biotic factors in an ecosystem.

energy available to a consumer higher up the food chain will be much less than that available to its prey.

When plants and animals die, the energy that remains is used by scavengers, like vultures and smaller creatures such as worms. The large remains are broken down into smaller pieces that bacteria and **fungi**—the decomposers—can use as an energy source. The results of the decomposers' activity is the release of nutrients, which can be absorbed by plants, and waste energy, which is lost as heat. In this way, the energy from the sun is never destroyed as it passes down the food chain; it has just been changed into different forms.

The real world is much more complicated than a simple food chain, however. There might be a few organisms whose diet includes only one item, but that is not generally the case. For example, the eagle eats snakes, but it also eats many other things (e.g., squirrels, rodents, and rabbits), and those other things are part of food chains as well. A complex and realistic way of looking at these processes is through a food web.

A food web is a series of interlinking food chains and is much more complex than a singular food chain. In a food web, members can be part of more than one food chain. Food webs illustrate the interdependence of all biotic factors in an ecosystem.

Maintaining a healthy balance has a direct impact on food chains and food webs. If a toxic substance enters the web at any point, anything else that feeds off of it is at risk for contamination. If key organisms or multiple groups disappear, this can cause severe problems in food chains and food webs.

As chains move from soils to plants to animals to humans, it is not hard to see why maintaining a working system is important. If any part of these systems fails, then everything up the food web from that point is negatively impacted. This relates back to the renewability and nonrenewability issues of plant resources. If a system or multiple systems are completely destroyed, resources can become nonrenewable.

PLANT PROCESSES—PHOTOSYNTHESIS, RESPIRATION, AND TRANSPIRATION

Plants need water, sunshine, warmth, minerals, and gases in order to grow well and remain healthy. These components come from the air that surrounds the plant's shoots and leaves, and from the soil that surrounds its roots.

A plant is able to produce simple sugars (glucose and sucrose) using carbon dioxide from the air and water from the soil. In order to do this, the plant also requires the use of sunlight. Of the sunlight that strikes the plant, green plants absorb only 30%, and only 2% of this energy is stored. The plant's green leaves trap the energy from sunlight. Chlorophyll allows the plant to make food. Plants need energy for growth, movement, transporting materials around their bodies, and to make complex chemicals.

Sunlight is what provides the power to combine carbon dioxide and water to produce sugar. This food manufacturing process is called photosynthesis. During photosynthesis, the light energy received by chlorophyll is trapped in the chloroplasts, which have received water from the veins and carbon dioxide from the air.

A plant also needs minerals, such as nitrates, phosphates, and potassium. These minerals come from the soil. They dissolve in water and enter the plant through the root system.

The light energy splits the water in the chloroplasts into two parts: hydrogen and oxygen. During this process of making sugars, the plant forms oxygen as a waste product. The oxygen leaves the plant and goes into the air. Plants also utilize small amounts of the oxygen.

Photosynthesis is the first step in making food. Plants can turn simple sugars into other substances, including complex sugars, starches, proteins, and fats. Once the food is made, the leaves send it to other parts of the plant through the vascular system.

To stay alive, the plant's cells must break down food in order to obtain energy. This process is called respiration. Respiration is the opposite of photosynthesis—while photosynthesis stores energy, respiration releases it. Photosynthesis makes sugar and gives off oxygen. Respiration uses oxygen to break apart sugar.

Photosynthesis only occurs in cells containing chlorophyll, but respiration takes place in every living cell. In addition, while photosynthesis only occurs during the sunlight hours, respiration occurs both day and night, allowing the plant to continue breathing.

In a sense, plants breathe. In addition to giving out oxygen, they also use oxygen and give out carbon dioxide, just as humans do when they breathe. Respiration creates energy that the plant uses to grow and repair worn-out tissue.

The gases from the air pass through the stomata on the undersides of the leaves. At dawn and dusk, a plant's rate of photosynthesis and respiration are equivalent. They balance each other out, enabling the plant to make and break down its food at the same rate.

At night, plants respire and take in oxygen and release carbon dioxide. At dawn, the plant begins to photosynthesize. During the daylight hours, carbon dioxide is used in photosynthesis, and oxygen is given out. At dusk, photosynthesis stops, but respiration continues through the night.

Transpiration is the process by which moisture is carried through plants from roots to the stomata, where moisture changes to vapor and is released into the atmosphere. In other words, transpiration is the evaporation of water from plant leaves. Nearly 10% of the moisture content in air is released by plants through transpiration.

Although the process is invisible, through the course of a growing season, a leaf will transpire many times more water than its own weight. For example, a large oak tree can transpire 40,000 gallons (151,000 liters) per year. An acre of corn gives off about 3,000–4,000 gallons (11,400–15,100 liters) of water each day.

The amount of water a plant will transpire depends on where it is located and for how much time. Several factors can determine a plant's transpiration rate:

- *Temperature*: The warmer the temperature, the higher the transpiration rate.
- *Relative humidity*: The more humidity in the air, the lower the transpiration rate. This is because it is easier for water to evaporate into drier air.

Watching Transpiration

Although the process of transpiration occurs without our seeing it, there is a way to make it visible. Place a potted, watered plant outside, and slip a clear plastic bag over the plant and the top part of the pot. Secure the plastic to the pot so that the outside air cannot get in. Keep the plastic in place for at least an hour, and watch what happens inside the plastic bag around the plant. Water vapor is released not only from the plant's leaves but also from the soil and forms liquid water when it comes into contact with the plastic bag.

- *Wind and air movement*: The more air movement, the higher the transpiration rate.
- *Soil-moisture availability*: If the soil is dry, the plant will begin to wilt and transpiration will lower.
- *Type of plant*: Plants in deserts transpire less than plants in other areas in order to conserve moisture.

If a plant's roots extend into the ground below the level of groundwater, the plants can transpire water directly from the groundwater system. A plant's roots are usually above the **water table**, making the plant dependent on water supplied by precipitation. During a drought, transpiration by plants may decrease as plants attempt to conserve water. The amount of the transpiration decrease depends on the plant's root and leaf characteristics.

Plants are efficient recyclers. When a plant sheds its leaves in the fall, many nutrients are still locked inside the leaves. Before the nutrients can be released and returned to the soil, the dead plant material has to be broken down. Leaf litter (dead plants and fallen leaves) is broken down by animals, fungi , and bacteria. Earthworms and millipedes eat the dead plants. Fungi and bacteria rot dead wood. Over time, all that is left is dark brown, crumbly compost. All the nutrients have been recycled by organisms or have soaked back into the soil to be absorbed by new plants.

EFFECTS OF DISRUPTION

Human interference can disrupt the natural cycles of plants. Interference can come in many forms—the planting of agricultural crops is one way. Unwanted plants are removed, and farmers use various methods to produce large quantities of healthy crops as quickly as possible.

In a natural grassland environment, many types of plants grow together. When the land is farmed, however, the natural grasses are removed, and only the crop is allowed to grow on the land.

Most farmers spray **herbicides** to kill other grasses and weeds. But herbicides can kill other plants in the area, as well. Herbicides can also kill any wildflowers that could have grown in the area.

Humans also spray chemicals called **pesticides** to kill insects and other pests. Commercial pesticides are combinations of various chemicals. There are narrow-spectrum and broad-spectrum pesticides. Narrow-spectrum pesticides target specific pest species. Broad-spectrum pesticides target a wider range of organisms, which can include the pest species as well as some of the nonpest and beneficial species. For example, pesticides can kill the beneficial insects that are necessary for plant pollination. They also break the natural cycle of the native plants.

Today, in the United States alone, 661 million pounds of pesticides are used each year. Pesticides include a large range of products, such as bactericides (kills bacteria), insecticides (kills insects), fungicides (kills fungus), herbicides (kills weeds), and rodenticides (kills rodents).

Fertilizers are added to the soil when plants are grown as crops. When the crops are harvested, they are taken away instead of being broken down naturally so that nutrients can return to the soil. To counteract this loss of nutrients, humans add fertilizers to the soil. The downside of fertilizers is that rain can wash excess fertilizer into lakes and rivers, which upsets the natural chemical balance in these bodies of water.

Other human-induced disruption occurs during the process of urbanization. As ground is cleared in order to build homes, roads, or other structures, the native plant cycles are disrupted or completely removed, upsetting the natural balance. In order to minimize the impact of urbanization, one practical solution is to landscape with natural plants already growing in the area, rather than introduce completely different plants. Using native vegetation also minimizes disruption to the established food webs in the habitat.

Natural disturbances can also disrupt the plant communities in an area. For example, climate change, drought, and erosion can threaten, endanger, or damage natural plant communities.

DEVELOPMENT OF BOTANICAL RESOURCES

This chapter will explore plant diversity; endemic and introduced species; and the roles of inventory, monitoring, and public awareness. In addition, the mechanisms seeds use to disperse and the unusual things that can happen to plant biodiversity in isolated locations will be covered. Finally, the wonderful contributions from the development of ethnobotany are addressed.

DIVERSITY—WHAT IS IT?

Diversity implies differences. A diverse habitat contains many different species. Diversity is good for a habitat, because if one species dies out, others will survive and the habitat will not be lost. Over time, native habitats actually become more diverse than nonnative habitats.

But what is meant by *native habitat*? Or *nonnative habitat*? The concepts of *endemic species, introduced species,* and *invasive species* are also important.

Endemic/Native Species versus Introduced/Invasive Species

A native species is one that occurs in a particular region, ecosystem, and habitat without direct or indirect human actions. Every species of plant (as well as animal) has a home in some part of the world where it has existed for thousands of years as a result of natural forces and influences like climate, storms, moisture, fires, soils, and species interactions. In other words, native species are those that would naturally grow in the area. The populations of many native species have been reduced by human encroachment, which has destroyed many millions of acres of natural habitat.

By comparison, nonnative species are those that occur artificially in locations outside of their natural ranges. In other words, they are species deliberately brought into an area where they would not grow naturally. Nonnative species can come from other continents, regions, ecosystems, or habitats.

Endemic species are plants (or animals) native to a particular place and found *only* there. The greatest richness of endemic species occurs in remote, often undisturbed areas, such as islands, on mountain peaks, around desert springs, and in other unusual and isolated habitats. More endemic species occur in isolated places because, without interference, these places can develop unique and complex ecosystems. Because endemic species in isolated areas—such as islands—have evolved in relative isolation over thousands of years, they are extremely vulnerable to change brought about by humans and introduced species. When introduced species are brought in, they generally do not have natural predators within the area they are brought into. As a result, these introduced species can outcompete and outsurvive the endemic species, putting the endemic species' survival at risk.

Invasive species are introduced plants or animals that can take over an area and crowd or choke out native wildlife. Invasive plants typically grow and spread rapidly, which allows them to become established over large areas. Free from the complex natural controls present in their native lands (such as predators), they may have rapid, unrestricted

The silversword of Hawaii. This rare plant is a unique, endemic species found only on the crater of Haleakala volcano. *(Courtesy of the National Park Service)*

growth in new environments. They can also produce an abundance of seeds, have a high seed germination rate, have seeds that live a long time, and mature rapidly to a sexually reproductive (seed-producing) stage. Their rapid growth allows them to overwhelm and crowd out existing vegetation and form very dense one-species stands, which lowers the biodiversity of an area. If this happens and a virus or a destructive natural event affects that one species, the plants will all die out.

Botanists often refer to *natural areas* when talking about the different species of plants. A natural area is an area of land or water with predominantly native vegetation or natural geological features that is allowed to respond to the forces of nature without direct human interference. In other words, it is an area that has grown what it wants without humans planting anything there. The term *wildlands* is also used to describe these areas.

World Regions With the Highest Percentage of Endemic Plants

Ecological region	Country
Madagascar moist forest	Madagascar
New Caledonian moist forest	New Caledonia
Hawaii moist forest	United States
Madagascar dry forest	Madagascar
New Caledonian dry forest	New Caledonia
Hawaii dry forest	United States
Mexican pine-oak forest	Mexico, Guatemala
Fynbos	South Africa
Kwongan heathland	Australia

(Source: World Wildlife Fund)

Invasive plants are a big problem and a growing concern for botanists, ecologists, and other land managers because they are a threat to natural ecosystems. Aggressive invaders do many harmful things: they can block out sunlight to other plants; and they take the water, nutrients, and space that the native plants need in order to grow. They can change the soil's chemistry, making it harmful to other plants; change the levels of water the soil can hold; and make the soil erode more easily so that soil is taken away from the other plants. They can also make an area more susceptible to destruction from fire.

Occasionally, an invasive species can form a **hybrid** offspring with a native species and change the native species' genetic makeup. They can also introduce pathogens (agents of disease, such as a virus or bacteria) that can harm all the plants. Other invasive species can contain toxins (poisons) that are deadly to insects and other life-forms.

Invasive plants can also be harmful to the animal communities of the area. If an invasive plant crowds out a native plant that animals like to eat, and if the invasive plant is not a source of food those animals

Ecological Impacts of Invasive Plants

Reduction of biodiversity

Loss of habitat for insects, birds, and other wildlife

Loss of, and encroachment upon, endangered and threatened species and their habitat

Loss of food sources for wildlife

Changes to natural ecological processes

Alterations to the frequency and intensity of natural fires

Disruption of native plant-animal associations, such as pollination and seed dispersal

(Source: U.S. National Park Service)

The Effects of Invasive Plants

Compete with, and replace, rare and endangered species

Disrupt insect-plant relationships

Disrupt plant-pollinator relationships

Become a source of disease for native plants

Prevent seedling establishment of native trees and shrubs

Kill other plants by shading them

Reduce the amount of space, water, sunlight, and nutrients that would be available to native species

Increase erosion along stream banks, shorelines, and roadsides

Change characteristics of soil structure and chemistry

Change patterns of water flow conditions

(Source: U.S. National Park Service)

will eat instead, it is harmful to the animal population. This eventually affects the entire food web.

The Critical Role of Inventory, Monitoring, and Public Awareness

Because of effects over time, native forests are usually very diverse. Time encourages diversification as new species evolve to fill specific **niches**. Gradually, interdependence is created among species that coevolve together. For example, a bird may evolve to feed on certain insects. These insects may in turn pollinate only certain plants, which in turn create shade favorable to the young tree seedlings just beginning to grow. Because of this, scientists and land managers must take inventory of which plants are growing where, monitor ecosystems to keep track of new invasive plants, and make others aware of the problems that can occur if invasive species are not controlled. Once an invasive species is identified, land managers must determine how to control it before it upsets the ecological balance of the area and the food webs associated there.

SEED DISPERSAL—HOW THEY GET FROM HERE TO THERE

The success of a plant not only depends on the production of seed but also on the *dispersal* of that seed. Dispersal is the process by which plant species move into a new area.

In order to survive, plants cannot just drop their seeds. If they did that, the new seedlings would have to compete with the parent plant and with each other. They would be too overcrowded and would be starved of essential nutrients. It is important that the seeds are dispersed over a wide area where they stand a better chance of finding the right conditions in which to grow. Because of this, plants have developed a number of ways to increase the chance of their seeds being spread far enough away from the parent.

Fruit plants—the fruit contains the seeds—fall into three classes: (1) those that bear fruit during the summer; (2) those that produce high-quality fruits in the fall; and (3) those that produce winter fruits.

Mammals or resident birds usually eat summer fruit, such as strawberries and raspberries, so that they are dispersed in the same general area as the parent tree. Fall fruits are usually eaten by migrating birds and can be carried long distances. Winter fruits are an important food source for resident birds in the winter when all the other food is gone.

Because these fruits take a lot of energy from the plant in order to produce, the plant's strategy is to make each one count. Plants not only have unique seed dispersal mechanisms, but also have a number of ways to keep animals or birds from eating all of their seeds, which would leave no seeds to grow new plants from.

Many species make sure some of their seeds will survive by using a mechanism called *masting*. These species may go several years and only produce a few, or no, seeds. At random intervals, the parent plants will produce a "bumper crop" of seeds (a bumper crop is an unusually large number). In many masting species, all the individuals in an area will mast at the same time. Animals will not be able to eat the enormous amount of seeds produced, which ensures that some seeds will survive to grow into new plants.

During the years when just a few seeds are available, the animal population is kept lower in the area because there are not a lot of seeds to eat—making the mast years as productive as possible by keeping the animal populations smaller. Examples of masting species include conifers, hickories, beeches, and oaks. During mast years for oaks, squirrels and blue jays hide many acorns for winter food storage, but they usually cannot eat them all or may forget where they put them. As a result, oak trees can eventually grow from these places.

There are different types of seed dispersal mechanisms. The different mechanisms include wind, water, animals, mechanical/explosions, and fire. The mechanism used depends on the habitat the plant is located in.

Dispersal Mechanisms of Seeds

Dispersal mechanism	Seed type
Wind	Dandelion, thistle, orchid, sycamore, poppy, ash, maple, grasses, milkweed, elm
Water	Coconut, water lily
Animals	Burdock (bur), blackberry, cherry, apple, acorn, tomato, watermelon, pumpkin, cedar
Mechanical/explosions	Lupines, gorse, broom
Fire	Lodgepole pine, jack pine, old man banksia

The number of seeds a plant disperses is called its *population potential* because each seed has the capability to produce a plant. In nature, however, the population potential is never reached because the seed may either be destroyed or land in a place that would not allow it to grow (such as landing in an asphalt parking lot).

Wind Dispersal

Some seeds are carried to a new location by wind. Seeds and fruits travel the wind currents and gentle breezes with the potential of inhabiting a distant mountain slope or valley. These seeds are very lightweight so that they can travel great distances. For example, orchid seeds are almost as fine as dust. Others, such as a dandelion, have hairy growths, which act like parachutes and carry the seeds far away. Wind causes the ripe fruits of the poppy to sway, which causes the seeds to fall out and be carried by the wind. Seeds of the wolffia (the world's smallest flowering plant) can be transported by powerful cyclonic storms, such as tornadoes. They have also been found in the meltwater of hailstones.

Many plants have developed ingenious adaptations for wind dispersal. These adaptations can resemble parachutes, helicopters, and gliders. According to W. P. Armstrong at Palomar College, there are seven major types of wind dispersal:

- Gliders
- Parachutes
- Helicopters (whirlybirds)
- Flutterer/spinners
- Cottony Seeds and Fruits
- Tumblers
- Miscellaneous

Gliders include seeds with two wings that resemble the wings of an airplane. One species in the gourd family, called *Alsomitra macrocarpa,* inspired the wing design of some early aircraft, gliders, and kites.

Parachutes have an umbrella-like crown of tiny hairs above a slender, one-seeded fruit. These fragile seeds can become airborne with the slightest gust of wind and can travel across valleys and over mountains. Milkweed and dandelion fluff are well-known examples of this type of wind dispersal.

Helicopters—also called "whirlybirds"—are seeds that have a single wing attached to the seed. Like a fan blade or propeller blade, the "wing" has a slight pitch to it, which enables the seed to spin as it falls. Depending on the wind velocity and distance above the ground, helicopter seeds can be carried long distances. The spinning action is similar to the autorotation in helicopters when a helicopter slowly descends after a power loss. Maples, box elder, pine, fir, spruce, hemlock, ash, and legumes are all examples of plants with helicopter seeds.

Flutterer/spinners have papery wings that flutter and spin in the air and can be carried short distances by the wind. Whether they spin or flutter depends on the size, shape, and pitch of the wings, as well as the wind velocity. Plants with these types of seeds include the tree of heaven, the *bignonia* family, desert willow, violet trumpet vine, American and Chinese elms, and four-wing saltbush.

Cottony seeds and fruits include seeds and tiny seed capsules with a tuft of cottony hairs at one end, or seeds embedded in a cottony mass. Many plant families have this type of seed: the willow family, cottonwoods, the cattail family, kapok tree, floss silk tree, and the sycamore family. During late spring and early summer in the western United States, the cottony fluff from cottonwoods resembles newly fallen snow. Because it can be messy as the fluff collects on the ground, many parks and gardens only plant male cottonwood trees since it is the female cottonwoods that produce the fluff.

Tumblers—commonly called tumbleweeds—are rounded bushy annuals that were actually introduced into the western United States from Russia in the 1800s. Tumbleweeds are pushed along by the wind, scattering thousands of seeds as they roll across open fields and valleys. A single tumbleweed may produce 20,000 to 50,000 seeds.

Miscellaneous wind-borne seeds include the grass family, such as the mountain and plains grasses. The seed-bearing sections are carried short distances by the wind.

Water Dispersal

Fruits, such as the water lily and the coconut palm, are carried by water. Coconuts can travel for thousands of miles across oceans. For example, the original coconut palms on the South Seas islands (such as Tahiti, Samoa, Tonga, and Fiji) grew from fruits that were carried there from the mainlands by ocean currents.

Animal Dispersal

Some plants have appealing fruits that animals like to eat. Because the animal only digests the juicy part of the fruit, the stones and pips (small fruit seeds) pass through the animal's digestive system and are contained in their droppings, effectively moving them to a new location far away from the parent plant. Examples of this are apple and cherry seeds. Birds also like to eat the fruit, and they disperse the seeds to other areas through their droppings.

Squirrels collect nuts, like acorns, and bury them for their winter food supply. If they forget about them and do not eat them, the seed has the potential to germinate and grow into an oak tree.

Some fruits, like the burdock plant, have seeds with tiny hooks. These burs catch on the fur of animals and the feathers of birds and can be transported great distances.

Mechanical/Explosions

Some plants have pods that explode when they are ripe and shoot out the seeds. Examples of these types of plants include lupines and gorse. Pea and bean plants keep their seeds in a pod. When the seeds are ripe and the pod has dried, the pod bursts open, and the peas and beans are scattered.

Fire

In order to survive wildfires, some plants have adaptive traits that allow them to reproduce. An *adaptive trait* is a characteristic that helps a plant survive and make the most of its habitat.

Some plants have developed fire adaptive traits. The intensity of the fire (the fire must reach a certain temperature) is crucial to the seed's dispersal. The frequency of the fire is also important.

Many species of pine have cones that only open after a fire. These pines are called *serotinus*. Jack pines have cones that are held closed by a resin that is sensitive to high temperatures. The cones will not open to release their seeds until a critical temperature is reached.

The lodgepole pine—common in the western parts of the United States—is both *serotinus* and *free opening*, which means that when the pine grows in an area where there are frequent fires, the cones are serotinus, but when it grows in an area where fires are less frequent, the cones open and release the seeds without the need for fire.

ISOLATED SPECIES—HOW DOES THAT HAPPEN?

Endemic species are usually found in isolated areas, such as mountain-tops and islands. But how, exactly, can that happen?

What Exactly Is Inside a Cattail?

The cattail is an interesting plant in the group of plants whose seeds are dispersed by wind. One fuzzy brown cattail spike may contain a million tiny seeds. Each seed has a tuft of silky white hairs and is small enough to pass through the eye of a sewing needle.

When the fuzzy spike opens, the seeds are shed in clouds of white fluff that float through the air like miniature parachutes. A cattail marsh covering one acre can produce a trillion seeds.

Each plant also produces billions of wind-borne pollen **grains**. In fact, this pollen was used as flour by American Indians and made into bread.

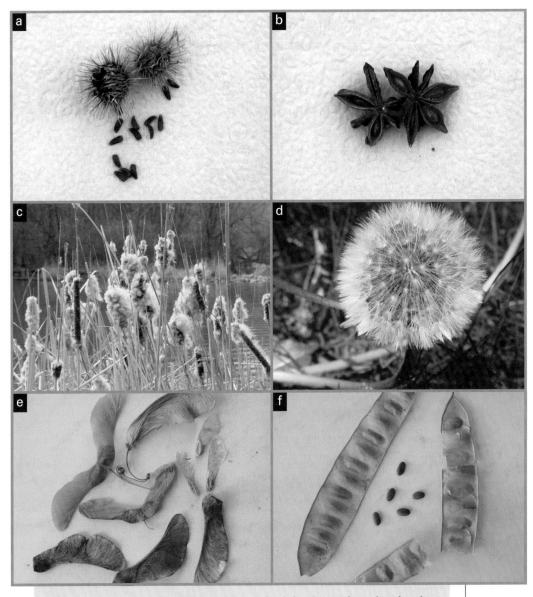

Different seed types have different dispersal mechanisms adapted to the plant in order to maximize its chances of succession. Principal dispersal mechanisms include animal transport, wind, and mechanical transport. Pictured are: (a) Bur–animal transport; (b) Star anise–bird transport; (c) Cattail–wind; (d) Dandelion–wind; (e) Maple–wind; and (f) Pod–mechanical. *(Photos by Julie A. Kerr, Nature's Images)*

Scientists have come up with the following four basic theories: (1) continental drift, (2) long-distance dispersal of seeds, (3) vicariance distribution, and (4) a combination of the continental drift and long-distance dispersal.

Because the continents of Earth are resting on giant crustal plates that shift over time, the continents have traveled great distances over the eons of geologic time. When two relatively isolated species are found to exist on two continents that were joined together at one time, scientists believe those matching populations occurred together before the continent split apart. Once it split, each new landmass carried a newly isolated community with it.

Some biogeographers (geographers who study global distributions of biological life) believe that many plants and animals are distributed in the patterns they currently exist in because of chance dispersal. There is a lot of evidence that supports this theory. For example, some seeds, such as coconuts, float in water and can be carried great distances across oceans to islands. Scientists have discovered seeds in bird feathers and in the mud on birds' feet from faraway locations that were successfully germinated.

Birds are capable of flying great distances. For example, a shorebird called a killdeer can eat seeds and retain them for as long as 120 hours. The killdeer can fly at speeds of 50–62 miles per hour (80–100 km per hour). This means that a killdeer could potentially disperse seeds over a range of more than 4,970 miles (8,000 km) in nonstop flight. Shorebirds can retain large seeds longer than small seeds, meaning that carrying these larger seeds is highly possible. This could explain species' existence on isolated islands.

Once a species inhabits an isolated area, it can evolve over time into an endemic species. As seen earlier, the silversword plant, found only in Hawaii, originated from a mainland herb.

Some biogeographers explain these various occurrences of plants with a theory called *vicariance*. Vicariance biogeography explains that a species distribution is determined by geographical and climatic events.

In other words, the movement of continents and climate patterns over time controls species distribution. If there are major shifts in climate from wet to dry, or cold to warm, it would determine which types of plants could grow in the area. When biogeographers study this, they collect data on plant distributions, plot them on maps, and try to find patterns called *tracks*. A common pattern of distribution for several groups is called a *generalized track*. This process is called *track synthesis*. Some biogeographers believe vicariance can only happen over short distances, however.

Many scientists combine continental drift with chance dispersal (such as from shorebirds) to explain present-day species distributions. They also believe there may have been interchange of species during the time the continents were drifting apart.

There is a great deal of debate between scientists today over species distribution and all the factors that control it. As geologic discoveries are made and theories developed, it provides clues for biogeographers as to how and why a species developed as it did.

The Remarkable Ecosystem and Amazing Plants in Hawaii

One area of the world that receives a lot of attention from botanists, biogeographers, and other scientists because of its large population of endemic plants is Hawaii. Hawaii contains many unique and fragile ecosystems where many rare and endangered species live.

Hawaiian plants began to evolve as much as 70 million years ago in nearly complete isolation. The Hawaiian Islands did not form from continental drift. They formed from a "hot spot" on the ocean floor that the Pacific Plate (drifting tectonic plate) slid over. The hot spot produced one Hawaiian island, then the plate shifted to the northwest, allowing the hot spot to produce another island, and so on. That is why the Hawaiian Islands lie in a linear pattern in the Pacific Ocean.

Because the Hawaiian Islands are located so far away from the nearest continent (2,400 miles, or 3,862 km), natural crossings of plant or animal species over the ocean to Hawaii are very rare. Over time, the few surprising arrivals of plants and animals have evolved into a unique biota, endemic to Hawaii. Plant seeds arrived on the winds, by floating, or attached to storm-driven birds.

Based on data collected by the U.S. Geological Survey, scientists believe that most of Hawaii's endemic species evolved from about 2,000 ancestors that arrived on the islands by chance. Based on the age of the islands, an average of only *one* successful immigrant arrived every 35,000 years. Some plant groups reached the geologically developing Hawaiian Islands much later than others, leaving a lot of opportunity for the earlier immigrants to evolve into new roles and habitats.

Scientists and nature conservationists today face challenges to keep mainland alien species away from Hawaii, where they can harm the defenseless island species. There are many plants that are unique to Hawaii. In fact, 87% of the **vascular plants** of Hawaii are endemic. The silversword—a beautiful flowering plant—exists only in the crater of Haleakala Volcano on the island of Maui. When the silversword is 10–15 years old, it grows a 6-foot (2 m) stalk that briefly displays magnificent blossoms before dying.

Unfortunately, today, there are currently more invasive than native plant species in Hawaii, brought in by various people. More than half of the remaining native flora in Hawaii have fewer than 5,000 individuals each in wild populations. According to the U.S. Geological Survey, there are 46 species that have only 2 to 10 individuals remaining in the wild, and there are at least 14 species that are down to only a *single* remaining individual in the wild.

ETHNOBOTANY—THE IMPORTANCE OF CULTURALLY SIGNIFICANT PLANTS

Plants have played an integral part in the existence of every American Indian tribe. Plants were used as food, ceremonial artifacts, and in

A Sampling of Significant Plants in Ethnobotany

Plant	Scientific name	Primary uses
American beech	*Fagus grandifolia*	As a dewormer; to treat skin problems such as poison ivy, burns, frostbite, rash, and scalding
Bloodroot	*Sanguinaria canadensis*	To treat burns, coughs, croup, sore throat, fever, stomach cramps, sinus problems, tooth plaque, and gingivitis
Chokecherry	*Prunus virginiana*	To cure colds, coughs, sore throats, chills, fever, and diarrhea
Eastern cottonwood	*Populus deltoides*	To treat colds, coughs, whooping cough, tuberculosis, bruises, sprains, and muscle aches
Jack-in-the-pulpit	*Arisaema triphyllum*	To treat headaches, snakebites, skin diseases, and open sores
Prickly pear	*Opuntia*	To treat bruises
Sassafras	*Sassafras albidum*	To treat colds, rheumatism, and obesity
Sourwood	*Oxydendrum arboreum*	To treat diarrhea, dyspepsia, asthma, tuberculosis, lung diseases, and anxiety
Strawberry bush	*Euonymus americana*	To relieve sinus congestion, dandruff, malaria, and constipation
White poplar	*Populus alba*	To treat muscle or joint aches, fevers, rheumatism, and gout (it contains aspirin, or *salicylic acid*)
White sagebrush	*Artemisia ludoviciana*	To help headaches, colds, sore throats, bronchitis, fever, smallpox, skin sores, stomachaches, and heartburn

(Source: Natural Resources Conservation Service)

medicines. Plants are also important in traditional American Indian lifestyles. This is referred to as *ethnobotany*—plants used for cultural purposes.

Over the years, the historical use of native plants has become of interest to many tribal peoples and also to the general public. The table on the previous page lists some of the significant plants in ethnobotany and what medicinal value they hold.

5

USES OF BOTANICAL RESOURCES

Because plants have the capability of producing their own food, they have been an important resource for animals and humans over the ages. Humans have enjoyed the benefits of plants over time for things like food, fuel (burning wood), shelter (homes), clothing, weapons (bows and arrows, clubs, spears), and even medicine. They were even used as footwear by the Mayans of South America, who collected sap from rubber trees, poured it in a container, dipped their feet in the soft sap, and let it dry. The result was custom-fitted rubber shoes.

In early history, when explorers began traveling to faraway lands, they took useful plants with them as articles of trade. Because of this extensive transporting, nonnative plants are common all over the world today. In fact, many crops that are grown today as staples origi-nally came from other areas of the world.

Today, plants play an ever-increasing role in our lives, whether it is apparent or not. Plants form the basis for the many diverse food webs that all life depends on. No matter what the food chain, there is always a plant or plantlike organism at the beginning of it. The study of plants that are useful to humans is referred to as *economic botany*. Plants provide people with environmental benefits, food, shelter, medicines, clothes, energy, clean air and water, many everyday household products, and even inspiration. This chapter explores the multitude of ways humans depend on, and use, plants.

ENVIRONMENTAL BENEFITS

There are many ways that plants benefit the environment. They help promote clean air and water. Plants are the basis of healthy ecosystems and have a major role in purifying the air and water. Because green plants harness energy from sunlight through photosynthesis, they provide valuable oxygen for humans and animals to breathe. They also take in carbon dioxide from the surrounding air, helping to minimize the **greenhouse effect**. Plants make up an important component of the water cycle, as seen in Chapter 3. More than 90% of the water that is taken in through a plant's roots is eventually released back into the atmosphere through the process of *transpiration*.

Biomass Production

Plants provide for biomass production. Biomass is plant matter such as trees, grasses, and agricultural crops. It can be used for many purposes. Humans have used biomass—or bioenergy (the energy from organic matter)—for thousands of years, ever since they started burning wood to cook food or keep warm. Even today, wood is still the world's largest biomass energy resource.

Through the advancements and developments of modern technology, other sources of biomass can now be used. Biomass sources include plants, residue from agriculture or forestry, and the organic component of industrial wastes. Even fumes from landfills can now be used as a biomass energy source.

Biomass can be used as a solid fuel or converted into liquid or gas for the production of electric power, heat, chemicals, or fuel. The use of biomass energy has the potential to reduce our greenhouse emissions. Although biomass generates roughly the same amount of carbon dioxide as fossil fuels, every time a new plant grows, carbon dioxide is actually removed from the atmosphere. Therefore, if biomass fuel was used exclusively, scientists believe the overall emission balance of carbon dioxide would be zero as long as plants continue to be replenished for biomass energy purposes.

There are several plant types that can be used for the production of biomass energy, including fast-growing trees and grasses called *biomass feedstocks*. An extra bonus in using biomass feedstock is that it provides income for the farmers that produce it.

Besides biofuels, other products can be made from biomass. Products that are currently produced from fossil fuels can also be produced from biomass. They are called *bioproducts*. Besides being renewable resources, they often require less energy to produce than petroleum-based products. Researchers have discovered that the process for making biofuels—which is releasing the sugars that make up starch and cellulose in plants—can also be used to make things like antifreeze, plastics, glue, artificial sweeteners, and gel for toothpaste.

When biomass is heated with a small amount of oxygen present, gas is produced in the chemical reaction. Scientists call this mixture *biosynthesis gas*. Biosynthesis gas can be used to make plastics and acids, which can then be used to make photographic films, textiles, and synthetic fabrics.

When biomass is heated in the absence of oxygen, it forms *pyrolysis oil*. A chemical called *phenol* can be extracted from pyrolysis oil. Phenol is used to make wood adhesives, molded plastic, and foam insulation.

Carbon Sequestration

Because the building up of carbon dioxide in the atmosphere has serious environmental consequences—such as the greenhouse effect—scientists are trying to find ways to reduce the carbon dioxide in the atmosphere (most of the carbon dioxide in the atmosphere is a result of the burning of fossil fuels to drive our cars and fuel other things).

Carbon sequestration is the ability to store carbon dioxide for long periods of time in plants, underground, or in the oceans, so that buildup of carbon dioxide in the atmosphere will slow or be reduced.

Scientists are experimenting with ways to remove this unwanted carbon dioxide from the atmosphere and store it in plants and soils, places referred to as *carbon sinks*. One method scientists are researching right now is to increase the capacity of deserts and degraded lands to sequester (store) carbon.

Erosion Reduction

Vegetation is an important factor in erosion control. Because the root systems of plants build a network in the soil, they help keep soil from being eroded by wind and water. Plants act as a stabilizing medium. One way that plants control erosion is by being a part of a wetland. A wetland is an environment where the plants live in **aquatic** conditions from damp soil to swampy, water-covered areas. Wetlands are ideal for absorbing water runoff from other areas and reducing flooding. They also make stream banks more stable. Wetlands also provide plants that trap sediment and hold soil in place to prevent erosion.

According to the U.S. Geological Survey, places that are prone to erosion include (1) newly constructed areas that have a large amount of bare soil, usually because the native vegetation was removed in order to dig on the land; (2) areas where wildfires have occurred and removed the plants that served as stabilizing groundcover; (3) areas that are always windy; (4) areas that get flooded; and (5) areas that have been subject to natural forces such as avalanches.

Many land managers choose to manually "reseed" these types of areas so that erosion does not become a problem. If vegetation is not planted to stabilize the bare ground, wind and water can remove large amounts of topsoil.

In mountainous areas, helicopters can hydroseed (lay a liquid-based seed mixture) and hydromulch (lay down a liquid mixture of straw) areas that cannot be accessed by truck. Areas of wildfire and avalanche damage commonly receive these treatments to control erosion and stabilize slopes to minimize the chance of mudslides or landslides.

Bare ground along freeways and other construction areas or hillsides are often hydroseeded by a truck, which sprays a greenish mixture of a blend of seed, water, organic nutrients, and a binding agent to keep it in place.

Bioengineering is another erosion control technique used at construction sites and naturally disturbed sites. It is a method of construction using living plants or plants in combination with nonliving or structural materials. This is a unique method of using biological, ecological, and engineering concepts to produce living, vegetative systems to prevent erosion, stabilize slopes, and even enhance wildlife habitat.

Another method of erosion control on slopes is to lay a biodegradable jute (rope) netting on the slopes. Anchored to the ground, it holds the soil in place while allowing the plants to grow up through it. When the plants grow, their roots help bind and stabilize the soil around them. The jute, meanwhile, biodegrades.

Wetland Restoration

Wetlands occur where water collects in low areas of the landscape. The plants that live in them are special—they must be able to adapt to changing water conditions and survive in the low-oxygen environment of waterlogged soils. As the plants die and fall into the water, the plant material decomposes slowly because of the lack of oxygen. Because of this, wetland soils contain a high percentage of partly decomposed plant material, called *peat*. Peat is what the coal used for heat today was formed from. Peat is rich in nutrients, which makes wetlands a suitable habitat for many different species of plants and animals.

Wetlands are areas of water storage because they act like natural sponges—storing great amounts of water and slowly releasing it. This helps prevent and control floods. Wetlands also provide water filtration. After being slowed by a wetland, water moves around plants, allowing the suspended sediment to drop out and settle on the wetland floor. Plant roots and microorganisms in the soil often absorb nutrients from fertilizer, manure, and sewage that are dissolved in the water. Other pollutants stick to soil particles, and the natural filtration process of wetlands removes much of the water's pollutants by the time

Wetlands provide homes and food for many types of animals. They are fragile ecosystems and can be easily harmed by human influences, such as pollution and urbanization. This photo was taken at Kanuti National Wildlife Refuge in Fairbanks, Alaska. Notice the moose entering the water on the right. *(Courtesy of the U.S. Fish and Wildlife Service; photo by Phillip Martin)*

it leaves the wetland. The natural process works so well that some land managers construct man-made wetlands in order to treat storm water and wastewater.

Water Quality Improvement

Water quality can be harmed by runoff from agricultural lands, urban areas, construction and industrial sites, and failed septic tanks. These activities contaminate the water with bacteria, sediments, chemicals, organic waste, and metals.

A group, or barrier, of plants along streams and around lakes, called a *riparian buffer,* is often used to control the pollutants and keep them from entering the water. A riparian area is an ecosystem involving rivers and the surrounding vegetation. The unique interaction of the soil, water, and plants allows the contaminants to be taken up into plant tissues, absorbed into soil particles, or modified by soil organisms. This "filtering" effect improves water quality in streams and lakes.

Vegetation plays a critical part in the health of a riparian area. Vegetation is important in slowing the flow velocity of rivers, stabilizing stream banks, and reducing erosion. Different types and species of plants provide different amounts of protection. Trees and shrubs are usually the best soil stabilizers and stream bank holders. Their root systems provide a deep, binding root mass and are critical in the development of overhanging banks, which provide habitat for fish and other aquatic organisms.

Plants are also important in the management of stream areas because they often provide the first indicators of change to the natural system. When plants are stressed, they can turn color, wilt, or begin to die off. This can alert a land manager that the environment has become unhealthy.

Coastal Dune Stabilization

An active coastal dune plant community occurs in the area between mean high tide and the furthest reach of storm waves, which extends to the top of the first dune inland. When plants grow on sand dunes, their root masses help to bind the sand and keep it from being blown away. The biggest challenges these plants must face are (1) high exposure to airborne salts, (2) sand blasting, (3) shifting of the sand, and (4) low water-holding capacity and low organic content of the sand. Because of these conditions, only certain types of plants can grow in these often hostile environments, such as beach saltbush, beach wild rye, beach bur and sea fig, yellow sand verbena, and dune grass.

Once sand dunes are stabilized by plants, the plants add organic matter to the sand as they die. Over time, the sand is transformed into a soil in which other types of plants can successfully grow. In these cases, a succession of dune plants to forested areas can occur.

SCIENTIFIC APPLICATIONS

Scientists often study the annual rings in tree trunks to determine what past climates might have been like in an area. Wide rings occur during years when there is plenty of rain. Narrow rings form in dry years. Trees grow quickest in the spring when the weather is warm but still damp. With this information, paleoclimatologists (scientists who study ancient climates) can determine climatic conditions over past time periods, and climatologists (scientists who study present-day climate) can use that information to predict future climatic conditions and trends.

FOODS AND SUPPLEMENTS

Plants provide the basis of food webs. Even the strictest meat eaters, such as lions, need plants because the animals they prey on are usually the grass eaters. Therefore, the lions are consuming the plants *indirectly* in order to live.

The food plants that humans eat today were once wild plants. They are what our ancestors ate before there were grocery stores. Horticulturalists (specialists involved in the science and art of growing fruits, vegetables, flowers, and ornamental plants) have just begun to scratch the surface of the food potential of plants around the world. In fact, many experts believe there are many more plant food sources in existence that have not even been discovered. Many of the plants likely exist in the worlds's rain forests and will eventually be discovered if the rain forests are protected and left intact.

Scientists have been able to breed plants and improve their food value by making them more productive and healthier. Scientists are able to breed food plants that are resistant to viruses, for example.

Fruits come in many shapes and sizes. They include berries; nuts; pods, such as those that cover peas; dates; pineapples; coconuts; papayas; mangoes; and many other types of fruits. The difference between a fruit and a vegetable is that fruit grows around the seeds of a plant to protect them, such as apples, oranges, peaches, plums, strawberries, and even tomatoes. Vegetables, on the other hand, are the roots, stems,

Annual rings in a tree trunk. Thicker rings represent wetter years, thinner rings represent drier years. Each ring represents one growing season—one year—allowing the age of the tree to be easily determined. *(Photo by Julie A. Kerr, Nature's Images)*

and leaves of plants. Interestingly, many people believe a tomato is a vegetable, although it is not.

When plants produce more glucose than they need for themselves, they turn it into starch and store it. Different plants store their food in different places. These storage areas provide a resulting food source for animals and humans to eat.

Carrots, potatoes, and radishes are roots. Potatoes and yams are also called **tubers**. Tubers are short, swollen underground stems.

How Plants Store Food

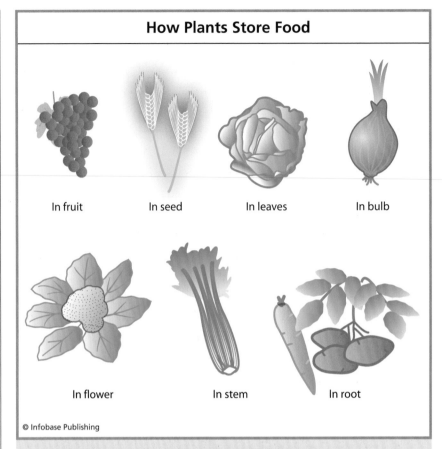

In fruit   In seed   In leaves   In bulb

In flower   In stem   In root

© Infobase Publishing

Different plants store food in different parts of the plant.

They have buds on them that grow into new plants (they are also referred to as the "eyes" on a potato). Cauliflower is the flower part of the plant. Beans, peas, and grains are seeds. Celery stores its food in stems and stalks. Onions and garlic store their food in **bulbs**, which are short, thick stems covered with dry leaves. Bulbs form from the base of leaves around the plant's stem. The stem becomes swollen with its supply of food. A plant is able to live off the food stores in the bulb during the winter months, which keeps it alive until the following spring.

Herbs and spices that are used to flavor foods are also plants or parts of plants. Cinnamon comes from the bark of the cinnamon tree. Some trees have a milky sap called *latex*. Chewing gum is made from the latex of the chicle tree, which grows in Central America.

Seaweed belongs to a group of organisms called algae (some of which are considered simple plants). They grow along rocky shores or float on the surface of the water. They are able to stay afloat because they have air-filled bladders on their strands. In some countries, such as Japan, seaweed is harvested as a crop. It can be used as food, fertilizer for crops, or as an ingredient for ice cream, toothpaste, and shampoo.

Sugars that are used to sweeten food come from plants. Simple sugars, known as monosaccharides, that are derived from plants include fructose. Maple syrup is a sugary sap extracted from several North American species of maple trees. Other sugars are extracted from sugar beets. Some plants are grown for the oils contained in their seeds, such as palms, soybean, olives, flax (the source of linseed oil), sunflower, and safflower. Vegetable oils are used in foods as well as soap. The coconut palm provides an oil that is used for margarine.

SHELTER

Plants also provide protection and shelter. Wood from trees is one of the oldest building materials and is still used in the construction of homes and other buildings today. Lumber is also used in heavy construction projects such as bridges, harbors, rollar coasters, and mine shafts. Lumber can be made from hardwoods and softwoods, depending on what is being built. Over 60% of the world's wood supplies come from the boreal conifer forests in the high northern latitudes of Russia, Canada, and Scandinavia.

Chipboard and particle board, used in the construction of homes, is made from shavings and splinters of wood resembling coarse sawdust. The wood is cleaned and dried. A resin is mixed in with the chips, which are then compacted into board.

Cork also comes from trees—it is the thick outer bark of Mediterranean cork oak. Cork is used for flooring and decorative wall tiles.

A log home nestled in the Uintah Mountains of Utah. *(Photo by Julie A. Kerr, Nature's Images)*

Plants also provide homes, shelter, and habitat for many other animals. For example, a single tree in the tropics can provide a home to more than 1,000 different insect species alone.

Cotton and other fiber plants provide humans with the materials used to make many of the clothes produced today. For centuries, people have worn clothes made of cotton and linen, which are natural plant fibers. Cotton comes from the white fibers that surround the seeds of the cotton plant. After the seed capsules are picked, the seeds and husks are removed, the longer fibers are spun into yarn, and the shorter fibers are used for cotton wool. Linen comes from the fibers of the flax plant. Throughout the world, millions of people are employed in the growing of fiber plants, and major industries are based on processing the fibers into yarns and textile fabrics.

MEDICINE AND HEALTH CARE

Many of the miracle medical cures now taken for granted originated from plants. As seen in the last chapter on ethnobotany, Americans Indians have used more than 2,000 wild plants for medicine. More than one-fourth of all prescription drugs today have plant origins. For example, aspirin was first discovered from a chemical called salicylic acid, which is found in willow trees. Teas made from willow trees are used to treat sore throats, laryngitis, achy joints, stomachaches, diarrhea, eczema, hay fever, and toothaches. Willow bark can be made into a therapeutic mixture and applied to treat skin rashes, sores, and open wounds. Emergency bandages can be made from sphagnum moss because it grows in acidic water with few bacteria, making it sterile and safe to use.

Rose hips, produced on rose plants, have proved helpful in maintaining good health. Because they contain up to 100 times more vitamin C than any food, they have been used to make vitamins and other products that work to prevent colds and other illnesses. Many people also use them to promote bladder and kidney health.

Quinine, which is used to treat malaria, comes from the bark of the cinchona tree found in the Andes. Some sedatives and substances used to dilate the pupils of the eye are derived from members of the nightshade family. Eucalyptus oil, from bluegum trees in Australia, is used to treat head colds and ease breathing. Morphine, a very powerful painkiller, is made from the sap of opium poppies.

Although many drugs are made artificially today, several still come from the original plant source, which is cultivated to produce it more cheaply and efficiently than a factory can. The next chapter on the importance of plants will discuss medicinal applications in greater detail.

ENERGY APPLICATIONS

Plants provide the oldest fuel in the world—wood. Prehistoric peoples who first used fire used wood. Today, many people in poorer nations rely on wood for cooking and heat. Some trees are planted as a crop and harvested for firewood.

Every time the lights are turned on in a room, plants that lived a long time ago are being utilized. Over 350 million years ago, giant relatives of today's ferns and horsetails were covered with mud as they died. This prevented them from decaying. Over the years, they were compressed to form coal and other fossil fuels, on which most of the world now relies for energy. The stalks of **cereals** and the remains of crops like cotton and coffee can also be used as a source of fuel.

As seen earlier in the discussion of biomass production, plants can be used to produce fuels as energy sources. Palm oils can be blended with diesel. Sugarcane can produce **alcohol** as a fuel with which to operate cars. The petrol plant, which grows in tropical regions, produces a sap that can be converted into a gasoline-like liquid. Scientists are working on producing a fuel from it that will be efficient enough to use in cars in the future. Ethanol is made by fermenting sugars or starch. Methyl alcohol can be added to gasoline to produce "gasohol" as a liquid fuel for cars.

INDUSTRIAL PRODUCTS

Humans make extensive use of raw materials and chemicals derived from plants. Plants and parts of plants are used to make many products that humans use every day. Corn alone supplies the ingredients for products such as fuel, pencil erasers, soap, glue, nail polish remover, bath powder, and plastic.

As seen with shelter, wood provides lumber with which to build homes. Timber from conifers is also used to make furniture. Wood is used to manufacture paper—a commodity that changed the course of civilization.

One-third of the world's timber is processed into wood pulp, which is used to make paper and board. Wood has to be converted into pulp first because the woody tissue is not pure fiber. It is a compound of cellulose (49%); **lignin** (21%); hemicellulose (15%); as well as small amounts of minerals, protein, and nitrogen. The cellulose fibers are separated from the lignin that binds them so that they can be processed into a material soft enough to make into paper products. Cellulose is also used in the production of methanol and other alcohols that are used as fuels.

Paper products can also be recycled. They become the raw material to reproduce paper again. Recycling saves money and energy, and it helps the environment because other trees do not need to be cut down. Today, about one-fifth of the production of paper in the United States is recycled.

Another important plant extract is rubber, which is produced by some species of tropical and subtropical plants. Rubber is composed of solids that are suspended in a milky fluid, called latex, which is found in the inner part of the bark.

Most of the world's natural rubber comes from Malaysia and the Far East and is used to produce car tires. In 1844, American inventor Charles Goodyear invented a process called *vulcanization*, which blends raw rubber with sulfur so that it is strong and remains durable under many different temperatures.

Rubber products are also used for carpet backing, footwear, erasers, hoses, tubes, balloons, raincoats, rafts, and many other products. Latex is used to make rubber gloves and catheters.

Before the development of synthetic dyes, plants were a major source of colorants for dyes, inks, and paints. Dye plants were grown as farm crops. They include indigo (a deep blue dye), woad, madder (red dye), henna (a reddish-brown dye used on hair, skin, and fingernails), safflower petals (a red dye used to make the cosmetic rouge), and autumn crocus (a yellow *pigment* used to color textiles and food products), to name a few.

Musical instruments such as guitars, violins, and cellos are also made from wood. Even the black keys on a piano are made from a hardwood called ebony.

One fruit, called a loofah, is commonly used as a sponge to bathe with. Although it resembles a sponge, it does not come from the sea. It is the fruit of a plant similar to a squash. The ripe fruits are picked and soaked in water until the outer layers break apart. The remaining fruit is dried and bleached.

The oil palm that grows in western Africa produces an edible oil that can also be used in a variety of other products, such as soap, lubricating oil, and tallow for candles. Cellophane, a transparent material used to wrap candies and packages in, is a by-product produced from the cellulose in plants.

Plant fibers are used in the production of many different types of rope. The fibers come from the leaves or stems. Usually the leaves and stems are soaked in water until the fibers can be separated and removed in a process called *retting*. Jute, a coarse type of rope, is grown mainly in India. Because it is easy to dye, it is used to make carpets, rugs, sacks, and burlap. Besides jute, other plants whose fibers are used to make rope products are Manila hemp, Indian hemp, sisal, ramie, raffia palm, and flax.

Roses, along with other fragrant plants, contain special oils that can be made into perfumes. These same oils are also used in lotions and ointments.

INSPIRATIONAL VALUES

Another use of plants is something that cannot be produced into an object or measured on a scale. It is an intangible benefit of plants—inspiration. Plants have an important aesthetic value; humans value their beauty.

Imagine a world without flowers, plants, or trees. Plants are everywhere, and people interact with them every day, from watching tulips bloom in the spring to playing football, baseball, and soccer on lush, green turf. People enjoy the beauty of plants each time they go to a

A well-tended garden in Salt Lake City, Utah, provides beauty and solace for visitors. *(Photo by Julie A. Kerr, Nature's Images)*

park, picnic in the woods, and hike in the mountains. People come from around the world to view famous gardens. Many people find peace and solace in planting and tending their own gardens. Sitting in a quiet garden on a warm summer day can bring feelings of accomplishment and satisfaction that cannot be directly measured but are nonetheless priceless.

THE IMPORTANCE OF PLANTS

The visibility of plants may be so natural that sometimes it is easy to forget the important role they play in our lives every day. Every time someone puts on a cotton shirt, eats french fries, takes a breath of air, takes an aspirin, or builds a new home, plants have had an effect on our lives. Plants play an extremely important role in what people eat, wear, and live in and also provide for our health and well-being. And they affect people not only in the United States, but all over the world. This chapter examines the importance of the goods and services people receive from plants, the critical sources of medicine plants provide, the role of cross-breeding and plant genetics, aesthetic values, biofuels, recreational opportunities, effects on animal habitat, wilderness survival, the role plants have had on the outcome of world history, and finally, ecological issues.

GOODS AND SERVICES

There are many goods and services that result from plants, including both tangible and intangible varieties. Tangible goods are items that can be picked up and physically felt. These are the plants people trade, buy, and sell. Tangible plant goods include grains, fruits, vegetables, flowers, fabric made from cotton, furniture, medication, and energy sources.

Tangible services include employment opportunities in many types of businesses. They provide jobs for scientists, farmers, clothing manufacturers, building suppliers, horticulturists, florists, landscape architects, chemists, biologists, pharmacologists, land managers, and many more.

There are also intangible goods and services associated with plants. These are the things that cannot be touched. They are the more abstract benefits that people often neglect to think about.

Intangible items include the addition of oxygen to the atmosphere for us to breathe, the foundation of food webs, habitat for wildlife, biodiversity, recreational opportunities, scenic landscapes, and natural beauty to look at.

MEDICINAL RESOURCES

Plants have always been a major source of medicine. By trial and error, early humans discovered that many plants could cure diseases, reduce pain, and help heal wounds. During the Middle Ages, apothecaries were like today's drugstores and pharmacies. Their medicines were usually dried plants and herbs instead of pills. The dosages were carefully measured, but the correct and safe dosages were not always known—they were not sure how much it took to cure, or kill. Fortunately, scientists today know much more about the chemistry of medicinal resources and their interactions with the human body.

In the past, herbalists (people who developed medicinal applications for plants) kept detailed records of herbal treatments so they could figure out the right dosages (too much of some plant ingredients could kill a patient). Today, pharmaceutical laboratories analyze these medications in laboratories. Because of scientific advances, many medications are produced today in a laboratory using chemical compounds that mirror the chemical structure of the original plants in order to meet the world's growing demands. Some medications, however, still use the plant itself. A concern for conservationists is not to harvest plants from the wild to the point of threatening them, endangering them, or causing their extinction.

Without plants, most medicines people take today would not exist. According to the U.S. Food and Drug Administration, over 40% of medicines now prescribed in the United States contain chemicals derived from plants. Historically, plant medicines were discovered by trial and error. This process still continues today. Botanists and chemists search the plant kingdom worldwide for new medicines.

Testing all the plants on Earth for medicinal value is a huge task. Of the estimated 250,000 plant species existing on Earth, currently only 2% have been thoroughly screened for chemicals with potential medicinal use. Because native plant habitats are destroyed almost daily, many plants that may be valuable for their medicinal qualities will be gone before scientists can even investigate them. Many scientists wonder just how many species have already been lost as well as how many are out there waiting to be discovered.

As seen earlier in the discussion of ethnobotany, American Indian tribes relied heavily on the medicinal uses of plants. Over time, this practice of herbal medicine has grown more complex. Science has enabled scientists to process these natural substances into pills, ointments, and powders.

Today, there is about a 25% chance that a medicinal product from a pharmacy—prescription and nonprescription—owes its origin in some way or another to plants and animals of the tropical forests.

Herbal Medicine

Herbal medicine, or green medicine, refers to the use of any plant's seeds, berries, roots, leaves, bark, or flowers for medicinal purposes. In many countries, especially those where doctors or hospitals are not available, some medicines are still made directly from plants. The World Health Organization estimates that about 80% of the people in the world rely on herbal medicines for some part of their primary health care. In the Amazon, forest-dwelling Indians use about 1,300 different plant species for medicines. In Southeast Asia, traditional healers use roughly 6,500 plants in treatments for diseases such as malaria and stomach ulcers. Many of these plant species are found nowhere else on Earth.

Herbs and Their Uses

Herb	Use
Ginkgo (*Ginkgo biloba*)	Improves awareness, judgment, and social function in people with Alzheimer's disease
St. John's wort	Treats mild to moderate depression
Valerian	Improves sleep
Echinacea	Strengthens the immune system
Bloodroot	Reduces tumors; also an ingredient in toothpaste and mouthwash because it reduces plaque and gingivitis
Devil's club	Purifies the blood; relieves pain; also a digestive aid; used to control blood sugar levels
Eyebright	Improves sight and aids in curing eye diseases
Goldenseal	Treats respiratory (breathing) conditions
Lomatium	Fights infectious diseases, such as tuberculosis; also treats common colds and the flu
Oregon grape	Helps a variety of skin conditions, inflammations, and infections
Osha	Aids as a decongestant
Pink lady's slipper	Treats nervousness and eases tooth pain and muscle spasms
Wild indigo	Stimulates the immune system
Crab's eye	Relieves sore throat and coughs
Aloe	Helps acne
Garlic cloves (bulbs)	Treats bronchitis and colds, as well as lowers cholesterol levels and blood pressure

In the United States, herbal medicine is gaining popularity as up-to-date analysis and research show their value in the treatment and prevention of diseases, such as the common cold and controlling blood pressure and cholesterol levels.

For most herbs, the exact ingredient that causes the therapeutic (healing) effect is not known. Whole herbs contain many ingredients, and herbalists believe that it is probably several ingredients working together that produce the desired medicinal benefit. Because of that, herbalists often like to use the whole plant.

Herbs can help people with arthritis, cancer, epilepsy, meningitis, menopause, nausea, pneumonia, rheumatism, tonsillitis, tremors, and tuberculosis. Like any form of medication, however, professionals need to be consulted for correct dosages and treatments.

Medicinal plants are also being used to treat livestock. The use of plants to treat animals is called *ethnoveterinary medicine*. This has been growing in popularity because many people believe plants are less toxic, safer, and more natural than manufactured drugs. In developing countries, medicinal plants are usually more accessible than manufactured drugs.

Prescription Medicine

Because so many different species of plants have been historically used for their medicinal benefits around the world, western medical researchers and pharmaceutical companies take a close look at the therapeutic plants and their chemical compositions. Oftentimes, they are able to identify the effective chemicals and copy—in the laboratory—the same combination of compounds. The benefit of this is that once a medication is produced artificially, the plant is no longer in danger of being overexploited or threatened with extinction.

One reason that plants are such a good source of medicine is that some compounds perform the same functions in plants and in the human body. Today, there are at least 120 distinct chemical substances derived from plants that are considered important drugs. One area in which much progress has been made is cancer research. The National

Cancer Institute (NCI) has developed several ways to screen plants for the possibility of new drugs and active plant chemicals. One of the prime areas "plant hunters" look is in the rain forest. Today, the Food and Drug Administration (FDA) has approved seven plant-derived anticancer drugs for use. The plants that have provided these break-through drugs are the Pacific yew tree, the Madagascar periwinkle, the mayapple plant family, and a Chinese tree species (*Camptotheca acuminata*).

A plant called *Trichosanthes kirilowii*, a member of the gourd family found only in China, is being studied as a drug to treat AIDS/HIV. A species of sunflower in China, called *Artemisia annua*, is showing great promise against a drug-resistant form of malaria. *Senna alexandrina*, a plant native to Arabia, has been used for centuries as a laxative. Mentha, a source of menthol, is used in topical (placed on the skin) medications to relieve itching. It is also a mild local anesthetic and an effective agent to help relieve muscle tension.

Atropine from a plant called belladonna is used in eye surgery. Atropine enlarges the pupil of the eye. Ipecacuanha, which comes from a plant in Brazil, is used if someone accidentally swallows something poisonous. Ipecac syrup makes them vomit to get rid of the poison.

Opium poppy is the source for the potent painkiller morphine. Purple foxglove is used as a cardiac (heart) drug, which increases the strength of the heartbeat. It is used to treat heart failure and other cardiac problems. Curare is used as a drug in general anesthesia. The Madagascar periwinkle is used to treat Hodgkin's disease and pediatric leukemia. Ergot is used to treat severe migraine headaches.

One of the most important discoveries was that of **penicillin**. In 1928, Alexander Fleming, a Scottish bacteriologist, discovered a mold with bacteria-killing powers so incredible it was effective even when it was diluted 800 times. The nontoxic mold turned out to have a high therapeutic value.

Efforts to produce penicillin in large amounts kept failing, how-ever. Then, in 1941, two British scientists brought the mold to the United States for further research. They got together with scientists at

Many plants are used for medicinal purposes. Purple foxglove (left) is used in heart medication. Poppy (right) is the source of morphine—a strong painkiller. *(Photos by Julie A. Kerr, Nature's Images)*

the Agricultural Research Service and discovered that the secret was corn steep liquor, which was familiar to agricultural researchers as a by-product of the wet-corn milling process. They continued to experiment with it and eventually developed a superior strain of penicillin, usually found on a moldy cantaloupe in a garbage can. When the new strain was made available to drug companies, production skyrocketed. Fortunately for soldiers in World War II, penicillin was available to treat the Allied soldiers.

Aromatherapy

Think of the pleasant aroma in your favorite restaurant or a bakery. The aroma (smell) alone can make your mouth water in anticipation. If you associate a loved one with the smell of roses, chances are each time you smell roses, you will be reminded of that person and will experience a warm, loving feeling.

This is how aromatherapy works. Aromatherapy is the use of plant oils that are believed to promote psychological and physical well-being. The aroma of some natural plant oils stimulates the brain to trigger a reaction and also provides physical benefits when inhaled directly into the lungs. Other oils that are applied to the skin can be absorbed into the bloodstream to provide the same benefits.

Aromatherapy can help with a physical condition or symptoms, affect a person's mood, or help relieve or temporarily eliminate stress and other psychological factors. Although aromatherapy will not cure serious illnesses—such as cancer—it can help improve a cancer patient's quality of life by enhancing the patient's mood, calming fear, and easing nausea during chemotherapy treatments.

Nature's Herbal Pharmacy

- In the United States, the market for medicinal herbs is worth more than $3 billion. Many of the plants are collected in the wild because the ability to grow them on large farms has not been developed yet. This raises serious conservation issues. If too many species are harvested from the wild, they could become endangered.
- There are at least 175 plants native to North America that are used in the nonprescription medicinal market today. An example is the ginseng plant. More than 34 million of these plants are harvested from the wild in the forests of the eastern United States each year.
- Today, more than 60 million people in the United States take herbal remedies. More doctors are recommending herbal medicines than ever before. In addition, some health insurance plans are now covering alternative health treatments, such as herbal remedies.

(Source: U.S. National Park Service)

Aromatherapy is not intended as a substitute for traditional medical care; it is meant to complement it. It can help with many common ailments such as cuts, bruises, acne, indigestion, PMS, hygiene, and inflammation. It can also provide mental and emotional assistance with stress, fatigue, fear, and anxiety.

Aromatherapy is not new—it has existed for thousands of years. The Chinese may have been one of the first cultures to use aromatic plants for well being. For instance, they burned incense to help create harmony and balance. Later, the Egyptians used oils and herbal preparations for medicinal, spiritual, fragrant, and cosmetic uses. Egyptian men used the fragrances and perfumes as much as the women did in their culture.

Later, the Greeks, and then the Romans, also used and enjoyed the benefits of aromatherapy. Use then spread throughout Europe. It is used in many ways today—from breathing eucalyptus vapors in order to treat congestion to airlines that provide warm, moist towelettes that contain the fragrance of oranges in order to instill in passengers a feeling of contentment and relaxation.

Aromatherapy has other practical uses as well. Some oils, for instance, act as a natural repellent and pesticide. One common product is the citronella candle that is used during the summer to keep mosquitoes away. Oils from lavender and peppermint are also natural repellents against insects. Sprinkling a few drops of oil near a doorway or window will help repel insects.

CROSSBREEDING AND PLANT GENETICS

In any group of plants, some will grow faster or yield more than others. Some will have better resistance to disease. Some will survive better under adverse conditions, such as poor soil and lack of rainfall. Scientists who work on plant breeding strive to select special characteristics of plants and to improve on these characteristics. Breeding is a very complicated science.

As scientists began experimenting with breeding, they were confused as to why the first generation from crossbreeding was uniform in offspring, yet generations after that first cross contained variations. Then, in 1900, the work on heredity done by Austrian monk Gregor Mendel (1822–1884) was discovered. He had observed the secret behind breeding and offspring, which is referred to as Mendel's Theory of Inheritance.

In Mendel's experiments, he worked with the garden pea. He crossed varieties with different characteristics—such as flower color—and counted the number of offspring of each type. From his experiments, he was able to calculate mathematical ratios. He assumed that

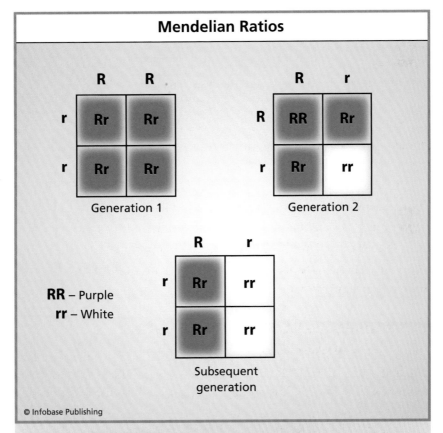

Mendelian ratios and resultant genetic combinations. These genetic interactions produce plants with specific characteristics. In this example, different genetic combinations result in plants with purple or white flowers.

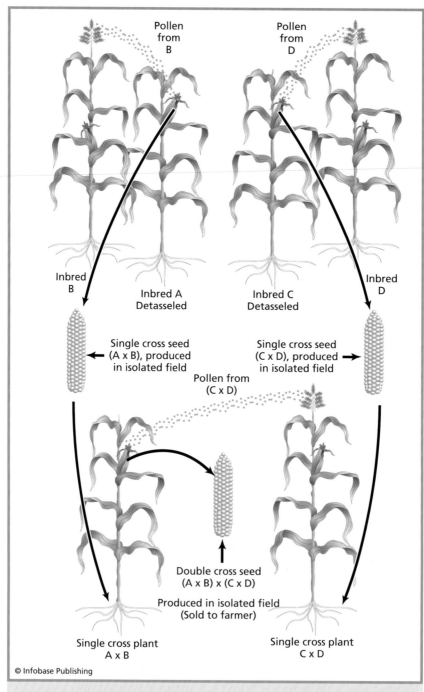

Pollen from B

Pollen from D

Inbred B

Inbred A Detasseled

Inbred C Detasseled

Inbred D

Single cross seed (A x B), produced in isolated field

Single cross seed (C x D), produced in isolated field

Pollen from (C x D)

Double cross seed (A x B) x (C x D)
Produced in isolated field (Sold to farmer)

Single cross plant A x B

Single cross plant C x D

© Infobase Publishing

Hybrid corn and how it is created.

each plant carried two "factors" to determine each characteristic, that one factor came from each parent, and that some factors would always dominate other factors. His theories accounted for the variations he was seeing when breeding his garden peas.

At this time, scientists began gaining an understanding of *genetics*. Genes—the factors carrying the information about the characteristics of an organism—are contained in the chromosomes of each cell. Genes are made up of DNA.

One cell from each parent combines to form a new cell. To avoid creating twice as many chromosomes as necessary, the parent cells go through a process called *meiosis*. This cuts the number of chromosomes in half, so that the new cell ends up with the right number of chromosomes.

New varieties can happen without warning, and the offspring can develop characteristics that neither of the parents had. This is called a *mutation*. Scientists have now discovered ways of altering the DNA of a cell. This is called *genetic engineering.*

Scientist Charles Darwin discovered that inbreeding (to breed closely related individuals) reduced the strength of plants and that crossbreeding restored it. This discovery is used in practical ways today in order to create stronger, more disease-resistant plants. Hybrid plants can yield up to 200% more than inbred plants. This is used in practical ways to increase the production of plants.

For example, both hybrid varieties of corn and wheat are used today. They produce larger crops that are more resistant to disease. This is just one way scientists have contributed to providing food for the world. Scientists are now selecting and breeding plants that can be used for food or fuel.

Aesthetic Benefits

The beauty of plants and the joy they bring to people are just as important as other benefits that produce tangible products. For example, giving flowers is one important, traditional way for people to express love, comfort, and cheer. Many people like to drive through the countryside

Outdoor gardens provide peace and solace. This is a backyard pond and wetland in Cantril, Iowa. Ponds are a rewarding way to practice conservation and provide habitat and biodiversity. *(Courtesy of USDA Natural Resources Conservation Service; photo by Lynn Betts)*

or hike in the mountains in the fall in order to see the changing colors of the leaves before they fall from trees prior to winter. These are the benefits from plants that are hard to measure because everyone has their own feelings and impressions about them. These aspects of plants create aesthetic benefits.

Leaves on deciduous trees turn from green to yellow, orange, red, gold, and brown, so that the tree can survive the winter months. If the leaves remained on the tree during the winter, they would lose more water through transpiration than the roots could absorb from the cold ground. The leaves would freeze and die anyway, and the energy the tree needs to survive would be wasted. In the fall, when it becomes

Topiary decorations are a popular part of many gardens. They can be many different shapes. This topiary is in Disneyland. *(Photo by Stephen D. Kerr)*

too cool and there is not enough light for photosynthesis to occur, the balance of pigments inside the leaves changes. It is the breakdown of sugars in the leaves and the chain of chemical reactions that cause the color change. The green chlorophyll is destroyed, allowing the reds, yellows, and oranges to show through.

Landscaping is another aesthetic benefit. From public parks and gardens planted for many people to enjoy to the landscaping and gardens people plant in their own private yards, plants add value to the environment. When trees are planted in yards and parks, they can provide valuable habitat for many types of wildlife. Trees can also help reduce home heating and cooling costs, help clean the air, and provide shelter from the wind.

An example of the artistic beauty of a carefully hand-cultivated bonsai tree.
(Photo by Julie A. Kerr, Nature's Images)

One type of outdoor landscaping technique that is growing in popularity is **topiary**. Topiary is as much an art form as a gardening technique. Topiary—which can be either indoors or outdoors—is the shaping of plants into identifiable forms such as animals and the shapes of other familiar objects. Sometimes, shrubs or hedges in public gardens or amusement parks are trimmed to look like an elephant, giraffe, bear, or a seal balancing a ball on the end of its nose. Those objects are called topiaries. Forming a wire frame into the desired shape, then planting it with ivy or another type of suitable plant, trimming it, and caring for it makes these magical shapes. Over time, the required care and trimming keep it looking like a recognizable animal or object.

People also use plants to decorate the insides of their homes. From potted plants to hanging ferns to flower arrangements, plants play a crucial part in decorating our immediate environment. The art of growing flowers and ornamental plants is called *floriculture*. One type of plant that is as much an art form as a decoration is *bonsai*. Bonsai is a small tree that has been dwarfed by pruning and trained over time into an artistic shape.

BIOFUELS

The past few years have seen a tremendous growth in the use of biofuels—such as ethanol and biodiesel—to replace petroleum-based transportation fuels. Two types, ethanol and biodiesel, are described below.

Ethanol

Ethanol production has grown significantly. According to the U.S. Department of Energy current U.S. production is about 3 billion gallons of ethanol per year for use in cars and trucks. Ethanol is a clean-burning, renewable product made from fermented plant products, such as corn. Because ethanol contains oxygen, it provides a cleaner and more efficient burning fuel than fossil fuels. When it is used in vehicles, it reduces carbon dioxide (a major contributor to **global warming**). Although ethanol does release some carbon dioxide when it is burned, the plants that produce ethanol recycle it.

Besides corn, other plants are being experimented with as sources of ethanol in order to increase efficiency. Methods to convert cellulose (the fibrous matter in plants) into ethanol show the most promise for the future.

Biodiesel

Biodiesel is a vegetable-based alternative to petroleum for diesel engines. It is a high performance fuel that can be used in all diesel engines to significantly reduce harmful emissions. It consists of 80%–90% vegetable oil and 10%–20% alcohol.

Like ethanol, biodiesel also results in a net reduction in greenhouse gases. It is also completely biodegradable; less toxic than table salt; and less combustible, which makes it easier to handle, store, and transport.

This unique custom-built treehouse is a form of recreation that involves plants. *(Courtesy of www.treehouses.com)*

As science progresses and technology improves, inexpensive and new sources of energy from plants will continue to be developed.

RECREATIONAL OPPORTUNITIES

Plants also play a huge part in recreational opportunities. Just about every type of outdoor recreation involves plants in some way. Whether it is hiking through the woods, camping next to a lake, going on a picnic and sitting at the base of towering trees, fishing, riding a horse through a meadow, bird-watching, mountain biking, building a tree house, or just sitting on a rock admiring the scenery, plants are a part of that experience and add to it in a way that nothing else can.

It is difficult to picture any kind of landscape that does not contain flowers, grass, shrubs, or trees. Many areas of the world are tourist destinations due to the plant life in those areas—for example, the national parks in the United States. Part of what makes these places so special is their natural beauty. And when people take the time to really look, plants are a big part of the picture.

EFFECTS ON ANIMAL HABITAT

Plants are also critical to animal habitat. Because plants are at the base of the various food webs, if something happens to damage the plant life, then the food that animals depend on will be threatened. If that food is no longer available, the animal will not be able to survive in the habitat. If the animal does not adapt to the change in surroundings, it can become endangered or extinct.

As illustrated before, it does not matter if the animal is an herbivore (plant eater) or a carnivore (meat eater). They all depend on the existence of certain plants in the habitat in one way or another. Many things can threaten a plant's habitat: drought (lack of rain), disease, invasion of weeds, overcrowding and competition with invasive plant species, urbanization, and misuse and mismanagement of the land.

Two different animals, their habitat, and the importance of plants to their survival will now be examined.

The giant panda's habitat consists of lush bamboo forests deep in a small section of northwestern China. The panda's home and food are made out of the bamboo trees. The panda consumes the branches, stems, and leaves of at least 30 different species of bamboo. Pandas also feed on other plants. As the human population in China has increased over the years, more space has been needed to support the growing population. The areas that are being taken to build villages are in the bamboo forests where the panda lives. As the pandas lose their habitat, they are subjected to starvation and death. The fewer trees there are, the less food there is available for the panda. Another problem with this is that the panda does not migrate—it stays in the same place its entire life. Once the forests are destroyed, its home and source of food are destroyed. A panda's habitat is completely tied to the existence of bamboo plants.

The koala bear is a tree-dwelling, herbivorous marsupial found in Australia. It eats the leaves of the eucalyptus tree. The koala is one of the few mammals that can survive on a diet of eucalyptus leaves. Because koalas live in societies, they need to have areas that are large enough to support many koalas. Koalas live in territorial ranges. The eucalyptus trees within their individual ranges provide them with food, shelter, and places for social contact. Individual koalas claim some trees; other trees are shared by many koalas. It is in the shared trees where the majority of social interaction takes place, making these trees very important.

Research has shown that socially stable koala populations occur only where there are favored tree species present. If the eucalyptus trees were destroyed in an area, what would happen to the koalas?

WILDERNESS SURVIVAL

Many plants that grow in the wild are edible. When people are trained in wilderness survival, that specialized knowledge can be used in emergency situations. Many scouting and outdoor recreation groups offer training in this fascinating area.

For example, a beech tree, common in the eastern United States, has beechnuts contained in their husk-like seedpods. The nut can be obtained by breaking the thin shell of the dark brown, triangular nut and removing the white, sweet kernel inside. The nuts are a good survival food because the kernel has high oil content. They can also be roasted and then boiled in hot water to make a drink.

Wild raspberry, blackberry, and dewberry—which grow in open, sunny areas at the margin of woods, lakes, streams, and roads—are often available. The fruits and peeled young shoots are edible. The leaves can be used to make tea.

The canna lily is a coarse perennial herb, which grows from a large, thick, underground rootstock. It is found in tropical areas along streams, springs, and the margins of woods, as well as in the wet, temperate mountainous regions. The rootstocks are full of edible starch.

Cattails are grasslike plants that are found at the margins of lakes, streams, rivers, and marshy areas. The young, tender shoots are edible raw or cooked. The rhizome is tough, but a rich source of starch. If the rhizome is pounded to remove the starch, it can be used as flour. When the cattail is immature and still green, it can be boiled and eaten like corn on the cob.

Chicory, a plant with leaves clustered at the base of the stem (resembling a dandelion), is found throughout North America, where it grows as a weed. The flowers are sky blue and stay open only on sunny days. All parts of the plant are edible. The young leaves can be eaten like salad. The roots can be cooked as a vegetable. The roots can also be roasted and pulverized and used as a coffee-like drink.

Dandelions, which grow in open, sunny locations throughout the Northern Hemisphere, are another food source. All parts are edible. The leaves can be eaten raw or cooked. The roots can be boiled as a vegetable. Dandelions are high in vitamin A and calcium.

Elderberry is a many-stemmed shrub with opposite, compound leaves. It is often found in open, usually wet areas at the margins of marshes, rivers, ditches, and lakes. It grows throughout much of eastern North America and Canada. The flowers and fruits are edible. A drink can be made by soaking the flower heads for eight hours and discarding the flowers. People in a survival situation have to be careful with this one, however, because all other parts of the plant are poisonous if eaten.

Junipers, sometimes called cedars, are shrubs or trees with very small, scalelike leaves densely crowded around the branches. They have berrylike cones that are usually blue and covered with a whitish wax. They grow in open, dry, sunny areas. The berries and twigs are edible. The berries can be eaten raw or roasted. Dried and crushed berries can be used in other foods as seasoning.

Oak trees are found in many habitats throughout North America. All parts are edible but often taste bitter. The acorns can be boiled and ground into a flour to be used for baking.

Pine trees are easily recognized by their needlelike leaves grouped in bundles. They grow in open, sunny areas throughout the world. The seeds of all species are edible. The young male cones, which grow only in the spring, can be collected as a survival food. The young cones can be boiled or baked. The bark of young twigs is also edible. Once the bark is peeled off the thin twigs, the juicy inner bark can be chewed. It is rich in sugar and vitamins. The seeds can be eaten raw or cooked. Green pine needle tea is high in vitamin C. Pine resin can be used to waterproof items. It can be used as glue. Hardened pine resin can also be used as an emergency dental filling.

PLANTS IN HISTORY

Throughout history, plants have played a part in everyday life and shaped the course of civilization. The castor bean is the seed of the castor bean plant. Its seed contains oil and is one of the oldest commercial plant products. Castor oil provided the fuel for lamps in ancient Egypt and the Middle East more than 4,000 years ago. Today, it is used in laxatives, cosmetics, and pharmaceuticals. It is also an intermediate product in the manufacture of adhesives and explosives. It is used in the manufacture of plastic; it provides lubrication for equipment used at cold temperatures; and it is an additive to soaps, detergents, and other perfumed products because it has the scent of jasmine. It is also used as the lubricant for civilian and military jet engines. It prevents the delamination and shattering of safety glass from temperature changes. It is used in shampoos, deodorants, and talcum powder for personal hygiene. Castor oil is classified by Congress in the Agricultural Materials Act of 1984 as a strategic material critical to the national defense of the United States.

In the 1600s, as the English and Dutch battled over control of the spice trade, a treaty was formed. In the Treaty of Breda, the Dutch—desperate to keep control of the spice trade—allowed the English to keep a settlement called New Amsterdam. In exchange, they got sugar-exporting Suriname in South America, as well as the island of Run in

Indonesia. Today, New Amsterdam is known as New York. Therefore, New York was traded for sugar and spice.

One of nature's most amazing items is the bark of the cork oak. It is strong, lightweight, resilient, fire resistant, insulating, capable of absorbing both impact and sound, and durable. After it is compressed, it returns to its original shape, yet it can be cut and sanded. The Greeks used it to make theatrical boots, whose thick soles elevated actors to stand like Greek gods above everyone else. Roman fishermen made floats of cork to keep their nets from sinking. Cork is most famous for being a stopper. Wineries around the world use corks in their glass bottles. A long-standing tradition, it became popular because the cork was such a good protector of the contents in the bottle. Because the cork was fitted larger than the opening of the bottle, the cork sealed the wine inside, and kept the air and contaminants outside. This led to a global market for cork—vineyards.

From the mid-1400s to the 1850s, the climate of the world cooled, creating what can be called the Little Ice Age. The climate affected the trees, which was evidenced in the annual rings of the tree trunks. Dendrochronologists (scientists who study tree rings) observed that the tree rings during this time period displayed less spring wood than summer wood growth. Some scientists believe this change in ratios of spring to summer wood may account for the tonal qualities of the violins made from that wood. Dendrochronologists have dated several of Stradivarius "golden age" violins to the Little Ice Age period. Not much is known about how the wood was cured back then, but some scientists have suggested that the wood was put in seawater for years, giving the wood a certain mineral content. They believe the addition of minerals to the cells of the xylem may have changed the resonance of the wood.

Kola nuts are the dried seed leaves of *Cola acuminata*. Native to tropical Africa, the seeds were purchased by Arab traders and taken across North Africa and the deserts of Arabia. Kola trees were introduced to the Caribbean during the colonial era because the plants traveled with the slave trade out of Africa. The kola nuts eventually made it to the Americas, and many years later became a major flavoring and caffeine source for the soft drink industry—and Coca-Cola was born.

These are just a few examples of the role plants have played in history. Their importance in our lives continues. Some day in the future, the current events now involving plants may be placed in the history books for future generations to read about.

ECOLOGICAL ISSUES

Many plants on the surface of Earth have become endangered, and many people have banded together to protect these species. Plants hold medicinal, agricultural, ecological, commercial, aesthetic, and recreational value. If endangered species are not protected today, they may not exist for future generations to see, enjoy, and benefit from.

Today, only a small percentage of known plant species have been screened for their medicinal values, although up to 100 species a day are lost from urban encroachment, poor land management practices, and natural factors, to name a few.

There are about 80,000 edible plants in the world. Humans depend on only 20 species of these plants—such as wheat and corn—to provide 90% of the world's food. Much research still needs to go into developing the world's food supply.

Plants (and animals) are the foundation of healthy ecosystems. Humans depend on ecosystems to purify their air, clean the water, and supply food. When species become endangered, the health of ecosystems is threatened. The U.S. Fish and Wildlife Service estimates that losing one plant species can trigger the loss of up to 30 other insect, plant, and higher animal species. How our ecosystems are managed now is critical for the future.

MANAGEMENT OF PLANTS IN A RAPIDLY CHANGING WORLD

The last chapter illustrated how important our plant resources are, the contributions they make to our lives every day, and why they should be protected and preserved. The key to being able to do those things successfully involves good resource management practices. This chapter looks at habitat destruction and loss; what happens when exotic species are introduced; the effects of disease, pollution, and overexploitation; the reasons for land use planning; soil management; the truth about invasive weeds; and finally, poisonous plants and their implications for each of us.

HABITAT DESTRUCTION AND LOSS

A habitat is a particular environment where both plants and animals live. As seen in the previous chapter, panda habitat is being destroyed at an alarming rate as the bamboo forests are cut down, leaving the pandas without a food source. This is an example of the delicate relationships that exist between the plant and animal components in a habitat.

Often, animals will adapt and remain in the ecosystem. They adapt to be able to survive on the food (plants and/animals) that exists there. Plants also evolve in habitats in order to be compatible with the animal life there. For example, some flowers give off a unique scent that will attract a specific insect and encourage it to pollinate the flower. The bright colors of some berries attract birds to feed on them.

Whole communities of plants are being destroyed every day all over the world, especially in the tropical regions. Rain forest habitats are being destroyed at an alarming rate in order to cultivate timber or clear the land for grazing. Firewood is often in high demand for cooking and heating in many areas, which adds to the already growing problem. Because most of the nutrients in a rain forest are contained in the biomass above ground (living matter, such as plants), the soil itself is not highly fertile. Clearing rain forest land often destroys it and keeps anything from growing and producing. Because the large trees take so long to grow, species are becoming endangered. If the plants are removed from the habitat, it adversely affects the animal life that depends on the plants for food, shelter, and survival.

Another threat to some plants is illegal poaching. Even though plants can be cultivated in nurseries, some exotic plants—such as cacti—grow so slowly that poachers take them from the wild so that they do not have to wait for a plant to grow over a long period of time in a nursery.

Good management practices attempt to take all the resources in the habitat and find a healthy balance to meet many diverse needs. Land managers must look at ecosystems on a broad scale, taking into account plant life, animal life, water quality, soil composition, air quality, different uses of the land, and human impact.

Responsible management for the twenty-first century includes employing practices that use the land to meet both present needs as well as protect the land's long-term quality. If one component in the system—however small—is damaged, it can impact and damage the entire system. That is why land managers monitor the health of plants and animals. If one of the components of an ecosystem is threatened, it is a warning of a possible domino effect. Wise management practices keep this from happening.

THE EFFECTS OF DISEASE, POLLUTION, OVEREXPLOITATION, AND INTRODUCTION OF EXOTIC SPECIES

There are many foreign influences that can affect the health of plants in an ecosystem.

Disease

Viruses are infective agents that live in the cells of plants (and animals) and cause many serious diseases. Viruses are so small that they can only be seen with an electron microscope. Viruses can reproduce themselves only inside the cells of a living host.

A virus is a simple structure. It is usually composed of a protein coat around a core of DNA or RNA—the genetic material that carries information from one generation to the next. When a virus invades a cell of the **host plant**, it makes the cell produce more viruses instead of more of the cell's own genetic material.

Viruses can reproduce quickly, which means that an entire plant can be killed, sometimes in less than 24 hours. In addition, the viral diseases of some plants can be passed on from one generation of the host plant to another. Viruses are usually transmitted by direct contact or by a transmitting agent. An insect can be a transmitting agent. If the insect feeds off a plant with a virus, it can carry the virus from one plant to another.

Once plants become infected with a disease, it is very difficult to get rid of it. Oftentimes, the diseased plants must be completely burned to get rid of the disease. For these reasons, environmental conditions must be monitored in order to make sure plants are being protected and remain healthy. This is why plants cannot be brought into some areas—such as Hawaii. If an infected plant was introduced into an area, the native plants would have no resistance and would be harmed by the disease.

Pollution

Sometimes water contamination is due to natural causes, and other times, it is due to human-induced causes. Scientists and land managers must look at water quality on the scale of an entire watershed (a region whose rivers drain ultimately to a particular body of water), not just small areas within the watershed. The entire system must be managed as a unit because everything is connected and pollution at one source can cause problems at another point in the watershed.

Water quality is a global issue. Maintaining high water quality is an important management issue because it involves environmental, economic, and health concerns.

There are two types of water pollution: point-source pollution and non-point-source pollution. Point-source pollution is when the source of pollution originates from a specific location or is a result of a specific activity. This type of pollution is much easier to correct and manage because the source is known. Non-point-source pollution is when the source of pollution comes from many areas at once. There is no obvious point of entry into the system. This type of pollution is much harder to identify and control.

Surface and groundwater can become contaminated with chemicals, salts, silt, and nutrients. Pollution can harm plant life, causing it to die off if it cannot adapt to the changing conditions.

Overexploitation

If plants are collected from the wild, this can cause problems—legally, economically, and ecologically. If the plant happens to be a slow-growing one, collection can deplete the supply of plants, causing them to become endangered and even extinct.

If plants are grown too intensively, it can deplete the soil of vitally needed nutrients and make the soil infertile so that nothing grows. If plants do not grow, there are no roots available to bind the soil, allowing wind and water erosion to destroy large areas. This is another reason for careful monitoring and controlled management.

Introduction of Exotic Species

European settlers to North America brought hundreds of plants from their homelands for food, medicinal, ornamental, and other purposes. This is how exotic species in this country were introduced. Introductions of exotic plants continue today. They are increasing because of the growth and mobility of human populations, which has brought increased international travel, as well as the accidental and intentional movement of many plant species between continents as a result of expanded international trade.

The problem with this is that many of the introduced plants have become naturalized across America, and some are replacing native North American species. These naturalized plants are exotic because people brought them from other areas.

If an exotic species outcompetes a native one, that can adversely affect the delicate ecosystem. Not all exotic plants are considered harmful, however. Useful food plants such as corn, oats, and wheat were introduced, but they pose no threat to natural ecosystems. However, each alien plant in an area means one less native host plant for the native insects, vertebrates, and other organisms that depend on them. Once again, everything is linked together in some way.

LAND USE PLANNING ISSUES

Good land management practices follow land use plans that have been carefully thought out. Because land can be used in many ways, it is important for managers to identify what those uses are and develop plans so that the uses can be compatible with each other without hurting the environment.

Some forests that supply wood for paper, building materials, and other important uses are managed forests. This means that their use is planned out ahead of time. The forest "farm" can be divided into different sections. One area can be newly planted seeds; another area may have young trees that can be used for things like fence posts; and other areas may have older, taller trees that can be used to build homes. By planning and managing this cultivation of wood, trees can be protected and taken care of while they are growing. Once they are harvested, the area can be replanted. This type of coordination keeps wild forests from being overexploited and damaged.

A trend that is gaining popularity in landscaping is natural landscaping. The use of native plants to landscape is beneficial because it helps restore areas to support the vegetation that naturally prefers to grow in those locations and conserves valuable resources, such as water. In other words, if grasses grow naturally in an area, those same grasses should be used for landscaping in the area. If shrubs grow naturally in an area, they should be used for local landscaping, and so on.

Native species are plants that occur in the region in which they evolved. Plants evolve over geologic time in response to the physical and biotic processes that exist in a region. For example, the climate, soils, timing of rainfall, drought, snow, and frost, as well as interactions with the other species that inhabit the local community, determine what plants will naturally grow there. Native plants have developed certain traits that make them uniquely adapted to local conditions. Because of this, they are a practical and ecologically valuable alternative for use in landscaping.

The use of native plants is on the rise across the United States as more people discover their benefits. Besides giving an area a natural look, they are also easier to care for because they do not require the intensive care and high water needs of traditional grass (lawn or turf) as a ground cover. More nurseries are growing and selling these native plants so that they are not depleted from the wild.

Botanists believe that using native plants instead of alien plants (plants not natural to the area) is better ecologically. Alien plants can hurt biodiversity. Due to a lack of natural controls such as insect pests and competitors, some alien plant species can easily become established in new areas. Once established, alien plant species can outcompete and displace the native plant species, disrupting ecological processes and degrading entire plant communities.

Some native plants may also be threatened if native/alien hybrids develop. Endangered species may be choked out by invasive plant species. Invasive plants can also clog waterways, disrupt groundwater flow, degrade water quality, and cause dramatic changes in native plant and animal communities.

Another benefit of using native plants is that they do not require the additional watering and fertilizing that alien species typically need in order to survive in the same area. Native species are well adapted to local environmental conditions; they maintain or improve soil fertility, reduce erosion, and require less pesticides.

Native plants provide familiar sources of food and shelter for wildlife. As natural habitats are replaced by urban and suburban development, the use of native plants in landscaping can provide shelter for displaced wildlife. Land managers can also use native plants to maintain and restore wildlife habitat. On a broader scale, planting native species contributes to the overall health of natural communities.

THE IMPORTANCE OF SOIL MANAGEMENT

Although there are many different types of soils, there are common factors that determine whether the soil is healthy. According to the National Sustainable Agriculture Information Service, healthy soil must have the following properties:

- It must be able to promote biological activity, diversity, and productivity.
- It must regulate water flow.
- It must filter, buffer, and detoxify both organic and inorganic materials.
- It must store and cycle nutrients and other elements within Earth's biosphere.

The concept of *soil quality* refers to the chemical, biological, and physical characteristics of the soil that allow it to perform these four critical functions. Soil is a working system.

The microorganisms (bacteria and fungi) and other animals (such as earthworms) in soils play an important role in getting nutrients to crops. They help deliver nutrients by decomposing soil organic matter and releasing plant nutrients. They also improve the structure of the soil by mixing and churning the particles, which serves to increase water flow to plants as well as to keep the soil's structure loose enough that plant roots can penetrate the ground more easily.

The level of carbon dioxide in the soil is also critical for healthy soil. This is called the soil respiration rate. The more available oxygen there is in the soil, the better. Oxygen becomes limited when soils are saturated with water. Soils with a looser structure encourage more oxygen circulation. In order to achieve this, gardeners often mix organic materials into the soil. They must also be careful not to overwater if they want their soil to remain healthy.

Other soil properties can be managed to create healthy soils. The bulk density, water holding capacity, and porosity (open spaces in the soil) can be improved. Bulk density is the combination of air space, minerals (inorganic materials), and organic materials. By controlling the soil's bulk density, gardeners can reduce soil erosion and leaching of nutrients and increase crop productivity. Bulk density determines the way the soil can store water as well as how much water it can store at a given time. If soil has a proper bulk density, runoff and erosion losses of soil and nutrients can be controlled.

Gardeners can periodically test their soil to determine its fertility. The following are the most important soil factors:

- Soil pH: An acceptable range is 5.5–7.8 on the pH scale (soils should not be too acidic).
- Fertility level: Fertilizers can be added to increase fertility.
- Organic matter: The soil should have 3%–8% organic matter.
- Salinity: The amount of salt in the soil and water should be low, or it will kill the crops (most crops cannot tolerate salt).
- Bulk density: Gardeners need soils with a good mix of air space, minerals, and organic matter.

- Water holding capacity: Crops do better in soils that can hold more water.

These are the factors that can be adjusted to make the soil more fertile.

When soil needs more organic matter, mulches or soil amendments can be added. A soil amendment is something that is mixed into the soil, using a tiller or spade, to improve the soil's texture or structure. Mulch is applied in a thick layer on top of the soil. Organic mulches help plant growth in many ways. Because natural mulches come from existing plant material, they decompose naturally into the soil.

Mulches keep the soil from clumping together. Mulch also protects the soil against erosion from rain or irrigation. Mulches keep the temperature of the soil under control. They act like an insulating blanket, keeping much of the sun's heat from drying out the soil. Mulch also keeps excessive water from evaporating, making sure the upper layers of soil have enough moisture. Common materials used as mulches and amendments include the following:

- Fir bark
- Chipped wood
- Compost
- Hay
- Bagasse (spent, dried sugarcane)
- Lawn clippings (dry)
- Manure
- Mushroom compost
- Peat moss

Researchers even use remote sensing (a science that uses images taken from satellites or photos taken from airplanes) in soil management. Images can be used to estimate the presence and concentration of salts in soil in specific areas. This data can be entered into a Geographic Information System (GIS) along with other spatial data (such as plant type, locations of streams and wells, and slope of the land) to build a scientific computer model to locate, monitor, and manage subareas and predict and correct localized problems.

Computer models can also be developed to evaluate, predict, and manage the movement of water, chemicals, and the movement of pesticides from fields to surface water and groundwater. By establishing working models, scientists give land managers tools to help them manage their land and conserve resources.

Researchers are also working with plant genetics to develop a better understanding of salt tolerance in crop plants that will lead to the development of plants that are more salt tolerant and easier to grow in salt-affected soils.

THE TRUTH ABOUT WEEDS

Native plants have evolved over millions of years to fill unique ecological niches. Invasive weeds are nonnative (did not originate in the area they are growing in) and have the potential to be ecologically damaging plants.

Invasive weeds are plants that developed in other regions. Growing in their own regions, they are not considered invasive weeds that harm the environment, because they developed within the local ecosystem. They are naturally controlled by competition with other plants and by insects, diseases, and other predators. When their population increases in the region where they originated, insects and other predators keep them under control.

The term *weed* is used to describe any plant that is unwanted and grows or spreads aggressively. An invasive plant is a plant that is growing where it should not be. A pineapple in a pumpkin patch would be an example of an invasive plant because it does not belong there, just as an orchid would be in a strawberry patch. Some invasive plants become a problem because they grow aggressively and crowd out native plants.

One of the greatest obstacles scientists and land managers face today in promoting ecosystem health is the rapid expansion of invasive plants. Some invasive plants and noxious weeds (which are harmful to human or animal health) can produce significant changes to vegetation, composition, structure, and ecosystem function. These aggressively growing plants destroy farming and wildlife habitat and can reduce plant diversity (choke out other types of plants).

Weeds know no boundaries. They are invading public, government-managed land; farms; forests; parks; and private lands. Millions of acres of once healthy, productive rangelands, forested lands, and riparian (river) areas have been overrun by noxious or invasive weeds. Weeds can dominate and cause permanent damage to natural plant communities. Scientists and land managers realize the seriousness of this problem and understand that if weeds are not controlled, they can damage the health of the land.

This problem is especially pronounced in the western regions of the United States. Because so much ranching and grazing of livestock occurs on either private ranches or public lands in the West, weeds pose an increased threat to the health of the land there. If weeds are allowed to take over an area and compete with native plants for soil nutrients and space, the native plants will die. Because livestock graze the native plants and depend on these plants for their food supply, weeds need to be controlled.

The same concept applies to farming. If weeds invade the fertile land and compete with the crops for nutrients in the soil and growing space, they will keep farms from being productive. Weeds can spread in many ways. They can be spread by human activity, birds, animals, wind, and water.

Early European settlers in North America unwittingly brought a lot of weed seeds with them. The seeds could have been hidden in the hay they brought over for their animals, in the dirt they used as ballast for their ships, in the fleece and hair of livestock, in their clothes and bedding, or accidentally mixed in with part of the seeds brought over to plant.

Some human activities, such as clearing the land to build on, or farm, created open places for weeds to grow. Settlers also purposely brought plants from their countries of origin to reseed areas cleared in their new land, make dye for clothing, or use as ornamental plants (as decorations). Some of these introduced plants may have become weeds.

When plants are introduced to a new environment, they may not have any natural enemies to keep them under control. Because of that, insects, plants, or other predators do not destroy them. Without any natural enemies, some of these plants become invasive (grow where they are not wanted) and lower the diversity and quantity of native plants.

The Facts About Weeds

Purple Loosestrife
- Each flowering stalk can produce 100,000 to 300,000 seeds *each year.*
- A small cluster can spread and cover a marsh in one growing season.
- Birds and mammals do not eat it, so if it takes over an area, the wildlife habitat is lost.

Knapweed
- One plant produces about 1,000 seeds that can remain viable for 8 to 20 years.
- The seeds are contained in a fire-resistant stem.
- Some people are allergic to it, and it can irritate their skin.

Leafy Spurge
- Seeds can germinate from 6 inches (15 cm) below the surface of the ground.
- Roots can be found 15 feet (4.5 m) in the ground.
- The milky juice in the leaves and stems is poisonous to most livestock.

Weeds are spreading rapidly in the United States. The Bureau of Land Management reports that in the western United States, weeds are spreading roughly 4,000 acres (more than 6 square miles, or 15.5 square kilometers) each day on public lands (lands that are owned by the federal government). They are also spreading on private lands, including agricultural farming areas.

Although some weeds have beautiful flowers, they can cause serious ecological damage. Weeds take over important habitat areas for wildlife, destroying shelter and nutrients, and reducing the number and types of native plants that can grow in the area.

- The seed capsules explode when they are dry and can shoot the seeds as far as 15 feet (4.5 m).
- The seeds can still grow after sitting for 8 years or more.

Tansy Ragwort
- This is toxic to horses and cattle, causing irreversible liver damage.

Gorse
- It grows rapidly and lives for more than 15 years.
- The branches have a high oil content, which causes a serious fire hazard.
- It produces about 8,000 hard-coated seeds each year, which are ejected by bursting pods and which can lay dormant (not active) in the soil for 40 years or more.
- Burning and cutting gorse does not get rid of it but rather encourages it to grow more.
- It forces the native vegetation out and is very difficult to control once it takes over an area.

(Source: British Columbia Forest Service)

How Weeds Multiply

In order to understand the severity of the invasive weed problem and the exponential explosion of weed communities, we will look at the rate of reproduction of *one* knapweed over 10 years' time. We will assume that 100 knapweed seeds are dropped in an area at one time. A knapweed plant produces 1,000 seeds per plant. Of the knapweed seeds, 4% will germinate (sprout) each year, leaving 96% for the following year's seed bank. Of this, 25% of the seedlings that sprout will survive to become mature plants. The knapweed seeds remain viable (able to germinate) for 8 years. It takes 1 year for knapweed to germinate and produce seed. Knapweed plants live for 5 years. The following table shows how many plants and seeds will be produced over the area in the next 10 years:

Year	Plants	Seeds
0	0	100
1	1	1,096
2	12	13,052
3	143	155,530
4	1,698	1,847,309
5	20,071	21,944,417
6	239,614	60,680,640
7	2,846,408	3,096,661,414
8	33,812,879	36,785,673,858
9	401,667,920	436,982,165,807
10	4,771,469,402	5,190,972,273,123

Now . . . that is a lot of weeds. Over 5 billion seeds in 10 years.

(Data supplied courtesy of the U.S. Bureau of Land Management)

When weeds do not hold or protect the soil the way native plants do, erosion increases, causing sediments to build up in streams. This in turn can hurt fish populations and water quality.

Some weeds, called noxious weeds, are a health hazard for humans or animals because they are poisonous. For example, leafy spurge can cause blindness, skin irritation, and blisters. Hemlock is poisonous and can cause death. Other weeds are hallucinogenic and can cause death, and many cause allergic reactions in people.

Weeds also pose a problem in controlling wildfires. Generally, they are less resistant to wildfire than native plants. Weeds also reduce the value of the land. They have a huge impact on ranching and agricultural activities because they can reduce the production of crops.

Weeds are a problem all across the country, and controlling them can be very difficult. Once farmers, ranchers, and others realize there is a weed infestation, it is usually big enough that it is hard and expensive to eradicate.

Biological control (using organisms such as introduced insects or diseases to reduce populations) is effective in slowing the spread of weeds, but it usually cannot get rid of all them. Farmers and ranchers can pull the weeds by hand or use machines to dig them up, but this is usually only done with small infestations. When farmers pull weeds, they must be careful that they do not accidentally spread any new seeds.

Herbicides are also good for controlling weeds and stopping their spread when they are found early. Most land managers use an integrated approach, involving a combination of these methods.

It is important in agriculture, ranching, and other activities to learn about weeds and get rid of them. A naturally functioning ecosystem can easily be thrown out of balance by an invading species. Controlling weeds usually involves the help of several people. It also involves awareness, detection, prevention, planning, treatment, coordination, and monitoring to solve the problem.

Examples of invasive weeds include purple loosestrife (in the eastern and western United States); spotted knapweed (in the eastern

Several types of invasive weeds. The spotted knapweed (a) was introduced as a contaminant in alfalfa and clover seeds from Eurasia. Yellow star thistle (b), morning glory (c), scotch broom (d), thistle (e), and butterweed (f) are other persistent weeds that land managers try to control. *(a, Cindy Roche, www. forestryimages.org; b, Peggy Greb, www.forestryimages.org; c, e, photos by Julie A. Kerr, Nature's Images; d, courtesy of Gil Wojciech, Polish Forest Research Institute, www.forestryimages.org; f, courtesy of Gerald J. Lenhard, www.forestryimages.org)*

and western United States), which can produce 1,000 seeds per plant and whose seeds can lay dormant for eight years; leafy spurge (in the northern United States), which has a powerful root system that can penetrate 25 feet (7.6 m) deep; yellow starthistle (mainly in the western United States); dalmatian toadflax; garlic mustard, which threatens native spring wildflowers); Oriental bittersweet (in the eastern United States), which is a twining vine that can smother trees and **saplings**;

water hyacinth, which clogs aquatic ecosystems; and melaleuca, a tree that has invaded the Florida Everglades.

The diversity of our native plant communities is decreasing, and weeds are damaging the ecosystems. As native vegetation is reduced, so is the amount of forage available for wildlife and livestock.

POISONOUS PLANTS

An amazingly large number of the world's plants contain toxic substances that can kill any creature that eats enough of them. Most poisonous plants never affect humans because humans do not try to eat them.

Scientists are not entirely sure why some plants are poisonous, because toxins do not play a role in the growing or fruiting process of the plant. The toxins sometimes serve as a protection against animals and people—another example of natural adaptation to the environment. Some plants even poison the soil and kill all nearby growth that could compete with them for nutrients.

Plants can poison by direct contact (touching it), ingestion (eating it), or by absorption or inhalation (breathing it in). They can cause painful skin irritations upon contact; they can cause internal poisoning when eaten. They can cause a range of interactions that range from minor irritation to death.

Sometimes, contact with a large amount of the plant must occur before any adverse reaction is noticed. In other instances, a small amount is sufficient to cause death. Every person has a different level of resistance to toxic substances. Some people may be more sensitive to a particular plant. It is important to learn which plants—both outdoor plants and houseplants—are poisonous because many poisonous plants look like their edible relatives or like other edible plants. An example of this is mushrooms. Some types are edible; others are poisonous. Poison hemlock appears very similar to wild carrot. Certain plants are safe to eat in certain seasons or stages of growth, and poisonous in other stages. Some plants and their fruits can only be eaten when they are ripe. Some plants contain both edible and poisonous

This figure depicts the diversity of poisonous plants. Always be cautious what you touch or eat in the wild. (a) Bird of paradise; (b) Tulips; (c) Poinsettia; (d) Pothos; (e) English ivy; (f) Daffodil. *(a, courtesy of Scott Bauer, USDA/ARS; b, d, e, f, photos by Julie A. Kerr, Nature's Images; c, courtesy of USDA/ARS)*

parts—potatoes and tomatoes are common plant foods, but their green parts are poisonous. Some plants become toxic after wilting, such as the black cherry. Some plants must be cooked in order to be edible because they are poisonous raw.

As a general rule, when out in the wild, *never* eat a mushroom or touch plants that are not familiar. Plants can also be poisonous to pets.

Plants that are poisonous when touched are poison ivy, poison oak, poison sumac, rengas tree, trumpet vine, and cowhage. The toxins of these plants are usually oils that get on the skin as soon as the plant is

Safety First—A Checklist for Poisonous Plants

The best defense against plant poisoning is not to let it happen. In order to do this, one must learn which plants are poisonous, where they grow, and what they look like. Never put any part of a plant in your mouth unless it is commonly used for food.

If there is an accident and poisoning does occur, it is critical to follow these important steps:

1. Call your local Poison Control Center *immediately*. You will be asked to give the age and weight of the person who has been poisoned, the person's symptoms, the name of the plant, and how much has been eaten.
2. Follow the instructions the operator at the Poison Control Center gives you.
3. It may be necessary to rush the victim to the hospital. Call 911 or the police for help in getting an ambulance.
4. Bring any uneaten parts of the plant with you to the hospital.
5. Stay calm. Most plant poisoning incidents are mild and can be quickly cured.

touched. These plants cause burning, reddening, itching, swelling, and blisters.

Plants that are poisonous when ingested can cause death. For this reason, plants should never be eaten unless they have been identified as being harmless. Signs of ingestion poisoning include nausea, vomiting, diarrhea, abdominal cramps, slow heartbeat and breathing rate, headaches, hallucinations, dry mouth, unconsciousness, coma, and death. These types of poisonous plants include castor bean, chinaberry, death camas, oleander, pangi water hemlock, rosary pea, and strychnine tree.

CONSERVATION OF CRITICAL BOTANICAL SYSTEMS

A s Earth's population increases, more land is used to build homes, construct road systems, farm, and alter the land to meet human needs. People must learn to use the resources that are available wisely. As land is converted to human use, forests have been cut and eroded, natural grasslands plowed up, and wetlands drained. As this has occurred, hundreds of plant species have been adversely affected. Each time a new shopping mall goes up or a new housing development is started, it changes the natural balance of the land. This chapter investigates habitat loss, wilderness and environmental protection, endangered plants and the Endangered Species Act, the effects of pollution, and the importance of backyard conservation.

HABITAT LOSS

Since plants have existed on Earth, many species have been unable to adapt to changing conditions. Thousands have become extinct.

When nature experiences a sudden earthquake, volcanic eruption, or flood, it upsets the natural balance of an ecosystem, but that balance is generally restored over time. The introduction of a new species can disrupt the balance, but before long, it either contributes toward the balance or becomes extinct. Unfortunately, the same is not true of human activity. Humans continuously upset the balance of any ecosystem they enter and reduce the ecosystem's natural diversity.

Any activity that reduces the diversity of plant life also affects birds, insects, and the other animals that depend on it, because the components of the entire ecosystem are connected. As these changes and disruptions take place, they threaten and endanger the existence of plant species. In the case of the rain forests and the huge amount of biodiversity that exists there, plants can be destroyed that have not even been discovered yet. These lost plants could possibly be the source of medicine to cure diseases or serve other important uses.

Many things can negatively affect habitat. For example, there are wetlands that have been drained, had their water polluted, and have been trampled and grazed. Being aware of the components of the ecosystem and having a working plan on how best to manage the land can prevent these actions.

Another concern is that the past and present use of plants for different purposes is leading to their destruction. As people become more educated and aware of their environment, they see a need to care for the resources and protect them. This process of protecting species so that they will continue to exist now and in the future is called *conservation*.

In addition to government organizations, many private organizations have been created to promote this conservation of natural resources—both plant and animal.

Plants are conserved in different ways depending on where they are located, how long they live, and the specific threats they face. The best form of conservation is to protect the plant in its natural habitat. In cases where the habitat is destroyed, however, the plant can be removed to a controlled garden. Sometimes plants can be protected inside a nature reserve in the wild.

The staff at the National Seed Storage Laboratory in Fort Collins, Colorado, preserves more than 1 million samples of plant germplasm. Here, technician Jim Bruce retrieves a seed sample from a storage vault for testing. *(Courtesy of the Agricultural Research Service, Department of Agriculture. Photo by Scott Bauer)*

Seeds from very rare plants are sometimes stored and collected in seed banks. This keeps them from becoming extinct. Once in a seed bank, the environment's humidity, temperature, and pressure are carefully monitored and controlled so that the plant seeds keep their ability to germinate for many years.

WILDERNESS AND ENVIRONMENTAL PROTECTION

One method of conserving and protecting plants and wildlife is by designating large areas of land as wilderness. Wilderness areas can be designated by various government agencies throughout the United States, such as the U.S. Forest Service and the Bureau of Land Management.

When land is designated as having wilderness potential, it is because the land displays some type of unique characteristic, such as rare plant species, unique animal species, unique ecosystems, or geologic and environmental beauty. When the government designates areas of land as wilderness, this means that it is protected from development and exploitation. Without protective measures, the resources could be depleted or completely destroyed, and many of them are not renewable.

Wilderness areas are protected from development of roads and structures, and motorized vehicles are not allowed. This ensures that the areas are kept as pristine as possible. Many government agencies, such as the Bureau of Land Management and the U.S. Forest Service, monitor activities in wilderness areas to ensure that the land remains unharmed. This is a form of good land stewardship—the concept of protecting the environment now so that future generations can enjoy it.

Wilderness areas are also off limits to potentially invasive and destructive activities such as mining. Invasive activities, like mining, can threaten the quality of water, recreation, and wildlife habitat.

Some of these special areas are designated as wildlife refuges. Associated with wildlife refuges are wildlife corridors. The type of wildlife and the food available, such as plants, determines a wildlife corridor. Many wildlife species have habitats that cover large areas of land. They establish their core habitats where human activity is limited, ecosystem functions are still intact, and wildlife populations are able to flourish.

However, many species have more than one core area and migrate from one to another, which ties in directly with the plants they require for food. Because of this, biologists often designate wildlife corridors to connect these core areas. This keeps wildlife habitat from becoming fragmented and enhances biodiversity by keeping both plants and animals connected. Federal government agencies that manage land are becoming increasingly involved in environmental management planning and monitoring in order to practice responsible environment stewardship of the land, now and in the future.

ENDANGERED PLANTS AND WHAT THAT MEANS

Because many natural habitats are being destroyed to make room for human activity, such as planting crops, building towns, developing industry, and constructing roads, many plants are becoming endangered. The Natural Resources Conservation Service warns that each minute 100 acres of natural forest are destroyed—and only 10 acres are replanted. Species of plants are becoming lost, and damage from erosion is increasing because plants are being removed and bare soil is left behind. When it rains, the water does not get absorbed into the ground—it runs off, washes away soil, and causes flooding.

Climatologists are also concerned about the rapid removal of plants from the tropical rain forests. They believe it will adversely affect Earth's climate. The rain forest plants release huge amounts of water into the atmosphere and absorb most of the sun's energy falling on them.

As plants are impacted, they can become threatened, endangered— even extinct. Currently, only a small number of plants have been studied to determine their usefulness to humans. But if they become endangered, humans may never know what benefits they may have had.

DISAPPEARING SPECIES—PLANTS IN TROUBLE

In the United States, there are many species of plants that are found nowhere else in the world—such as the silversword of Hawaii, which only grows in the Haleakala volcano crater. More than 20,000 different species of plants are considered native to this country, but environmental scientists at the Center for Plant Conservation have determined that one in every five of those plants may be in danger of disappearing.

One-fifth of the native plants in this country are labeled "rare." In order to be considered rare, a plant must meet one or more of the three following conditions: (1) a small population size, (2) a small geographic range, or (3) a small habitat. Plants can be rare for a variety of different reasons. Their habitats could be naturally rare, such as areas affected uniquely by geography or climate. They could also be unnaturally rare because of human influence, such as (1) development, (2) pollution, (3) invasion by exotic species, (4) development, or (5) overcollecting.

A species is considered *endangered* when it is in danger of becoming extinct in the near future if not protected. *Threatened* is a term used to describe species that are likely to become endangered soon, if they are not protected. *Rare* refers to a plant that is of concern to conservationists.

Rare native plants have an intangible benefit. Because they have evolved over millions of years, they have adapted their own niches in ecosystems.

The greatest threat to biodiversity is habitat loss and change. Recreation is having greater impacts on the environment today. Activities such as the increasingly popular off-highway-vehicles (OHVs) have created adverse effects in many parts of the country. Many fragile habitats, such as sand dune areas in Utah, Nevada, and California, which provide a home to dozens of native species, are being destroyed.

Many plants are trampled and destroyed by hikers, intentionally or accidentally. A policy that the Bureau of Land Management and the Forest Service promote is the "Leave No Trace" concept. This means that hikers should always hike on designated trails so that plants do not get broken or ruined. When in a natural setting, visitors should always make sure they leave the area untouched, looking like they had never been there.

Collecting plants from the wild to plant in private yards is also harmful. Laws have been established to keep this from happening, but it is an increasing problem. Collecting pressures threaten such plants as cacti, pitcher plants, and orchids because of their unique ornamental value.

Alien and exotic species can also have devastating effects on biodiversity as they outcompete or destroy native species. Some alien plants are intentionally introduced into the environment; some are unknowingly or accidentally introduced—but the negative effect is still the same.

About 4,000 plants native to the United States are of concern to conservationists and land managers. The green pitcher plant (*Sarracenia oreophila*) is a federally protected endangered plant that only exists in a few wild populations in Alabama and Georgia. Its limited range and specialized habitat make it the rarest of all pitcher plants.

A type of Hawaiian cotton, called Ma'o (*Gossypium tomentosum*) is close to extinction because of excessive land development on the Hawaiian Islands. Once used as a source of green and yellow dye by Hawaiians, Hawaiian cotton is important today because it is used to develop disease-resistant strains of commercial cotton.

A plant called Price's groundnut (*Apios priceana*)—once used as a food source by the American Indians—only exists in 25 small populations in the Midwest. Cattle grazing, herbicides, and clear-cutting (removal) have destroyed the plant's habitat. Scientists believe that if the loss of the plant's habitat could be recovered, it could be developed as a food crop in the United States.

These are but a few examples of the threat to plant populations today. Endangerment affects all areas of the world.

THE ENDANGERED SPECIES ACT

Many species, both known and unknown to science, are being lost forever. Even the lowest estimates put this loss at three species per day. If the human population doubles over the next 50 years, even greater pressure will be placed on the environment. In order to control the

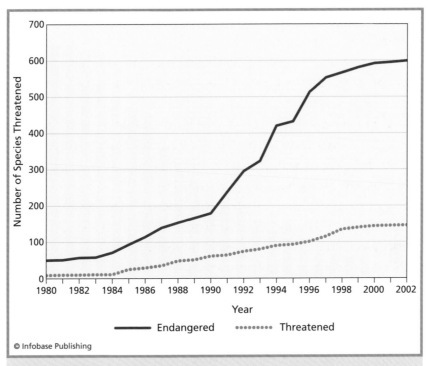

Trends of threatened and endangered species from 1980–2002. *(Source: U.S. Fish and Wildlife Service)*

trend of human-induced extinctions of species, laws have to be put in place to protect species—both plant and animal.

The first step toward conservation is education, so that people understand why there is a threat and what will happen if present destruction is not stopped. The U.S. Fish and Wildlife Service—part of our federal government—uses information from biologists nationwide to decide which species are threatened and endangered throughout the country. Identified species can then become legally protected under the U.S. Endangered Species Act of 1973. Under this law, all plant species that are placed on the list of Endangered and Threatened Wildlife and Plants cannot be exported or imported, sold without permits, or removed from federal lands. The penalty is stiff: Violators can be fined $100,000 and spend a year in jail.

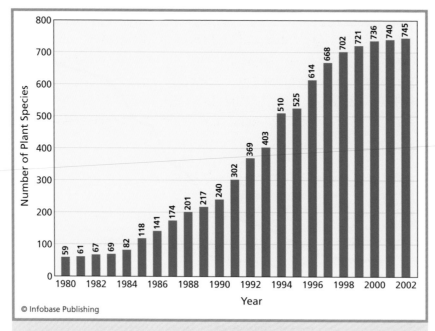

The total number of plant species listed as threatened or endangered from 1980–2002. *(Source: U.S. Fish and Wildlife Service)*

Individual state governments also have measures in place to protect plants, usually through the state's department of conservation of natural resources. Many private organizations also promote conservation. Several organizations operate botanical gardens (arboretums) that store and grow threatened and endangered species, in order to prevent extinction or promote ecological restoration, research, education and public awareness.

Species that are saved first are those that conservationists believe need immediate attention. They look at several issues to determine which species those are, such as type and extend of the threat, the cause of rarity, economic potential, geographic range, and number of existing plants. The biology of the plant, such as its reproduction, growth rate, and life span are also considered.

High-priority species often include endemics (plants that are native to one specific area and exist nowhere else on Earth) because these species are very susceptible to environmental change and are often indicators of unique and rare habitats. For example, about 90% of Hawaii's plants are endemic. Hawaii also has the highest percentage of endangered plants in the United States.

The initial concept for the Endangered Species Act of 1973 began in 1966 with the establishment of the Endangered Species

Terms Used to Define Endangered Species

Extinct	The last individual of a given species is dead.
Extinct in the wild	When a species only exists in captivity, not in its natural environment.
Critically endangered	A species facing an extremely high risk of extinction in the wild. This is used when: (1) 80% of the population has been destroyed; (2) its small habitat range is less than 39 square miles (101 sq. km); or (3) it has a 50% probability of becoming extinct within 10 years.
Endangered	A species facing a high risk of extinction in the world. This is used when: (1) 80% of the population has been destroyed; (2) its habitat range is less than 2,000 square miles (5,180 sq. km); or (3) it has a 20% probability of being extinct in the next 20 years.
Vulnerable	Species facing a high risk of extinction in the wild. Its population has (1) been reduced by 30%; (2) its habitat range is less than 7,800 square miles (20,200 sq. km); or (3) it has a 10% probability of extinction within the next 100 years.
Near threatened	A species that may qualify for endangered or vulnerable in the future.
Least concern	A species that, at present, does not face endangerment.

(Source: International Union for the Conservation of Nature)

Preservation Act. Unfortunately, the 1966 legislation listed rare and disappearing species without giving them protection. The first real effort to stop the loss of endangered species came with the enactment of the 1969 Endangered Species Conservation Act, which banned the import of species threatened with worldwide extinction. Then, in 1973, President Nixon signed into law the Endangered Species Act. This law focused on protecting species faced with imminent extinction. It focused on making the extinction of any species illegal. It banned the harming of listed species in any way, including the destruction of their habitat.

It is one of the most far-reaching laws ever enacted by any country. Congress established this act because it recognized that all species "are of aesthetic, ecological, educational, historical, recreational, and scientific value to the Nation and its people"(Endangered Species Act 1973).

Species now receive considerable protection from the government. When a species is listed, the government has the opportunity to identify critical habitat for the species. The government has the duty to seek the recovery of the species and save it from the risk of extinction.

Not only is it important for federal and state governments to take measures to prevent species from becoming endangered, but it is also up to each member of the community to do their part in conserving endangered plants.

After more than 30 years of having the Endangered Species Act in place, the result has been extremely effective. By focusing on protection of the species themselves, as well as conservation of the ecosystems on which they depend, our knowledge of ecological systems has expanded, and our understanding of protecting and providing for species has greatly increased.

THE TESS LIST

The TESS list (Threatened and Endangered Species System) is the official listing maintained by the U.S. Fish and Wildlife Service that identifies species that are threatened or endangered (see table on opposite page). The list is used to keep track of data, such as the historic range of the plant and how many individual plants existed in the population when it was listed.

The listing of threatened and endangered species must follow specific guidelines. In order to request that a species be listed, a petition must be entered. Nominating officials check the species against a

A Sampling of Threatened and Endangered Species

Threatened species	Endangered species
San Diego thornmint (*Acanthomintha ilicifolia*)	Pawpaw (*Deering othamnus pulchellus*)
Northern wild monkshood (*Aconitum noveboracense*)	Lakela's mint (*Dicerandra immaculata*)
Price's potato-bean (*Apios priceana*)	Black lace cactus (*Echinocereus reichenbachii*)
Manzanita (*Arctostaphylos pallida*)	Snakeroot (*Eryngium cuneifolium*)
Mariposa pussypaws (*Calyptridium pulchellum*)	Wallflower (*Erysimum capitatum*)
Navajo sedge (*Carex specuicola*)	Clay's hibiscus (*Hibiscus clayi*)
Ash-gray paintbrush (*Castilleja cinerea*)	San Rafael cactus (*Pediocactus despainii*)
Cory cactus (*Coryphantha ramillosa*)	Eureka dune grass (*Swallenia alexandrae*)
Lee pincushion cactus (*Coryphantha sneedii*)	Monterey clover (*Trifolium trichocalyx*)
Mountain golden heather (*Hudsonia montana*)	Texas wild rice (*Zizania texana*)

(Source: The TESS List, U.S. Fish and Wildlife Service)

Pollution from power plants and factories can mix with water to form acid rain, which threatens plant life and the animals that feed on plants.

database of North American species and review the information over a 12-month period. If listing the species is warranted, the scientific community, the public, and federal and state government agencies then review it for two months. Once a species passes this level of review, it is officially added to the list of species in the *Federal Register*.

THE EFFECTS OF POLLUTION

Plants need the right conditions in which to grow. The soil must hold the right amount of water and be able to provide nutrients the plant needs. It is also important that the ground be free from harmful chemicals that can seep into the water table and damage the plants when they draw the contaminated water into their roots.

Plants are also very sensitive to the quality of the air. Air pollution from factories and other sources of emissions can kill plants. Particularly hazardous are the effects of **acid rain**.

All rain contains minimal amounts of harmless acids because it dissolves natural carbon dioxide and sulfur dioxide in the air. The problem arises, however, when human activities become involved. Cities pollute the air with gases from power stations, factories, cars, and homes when fuel is burned. This puts large amounts of sulfur and nitrogen into the air. These chemicals then react with damp air to produce strong sulfuric and nitric acids. They can be carried large distances in the atmosphere and fall as acid rain, which kills trees and other plants.

BACKYARD CONSERVATION AND ENVIRONMENTAL USES FOR VEGETATION

One way everyone can help with the conservation effort is to create a backyard natural habitat. By choosing native plants that are suited for the area, little maintenance, chemical fertilizers, herbicides, or additional watering are necessary for the plants to remain healthy. It is not only easier to have a natural habitat, but it is also better for the wildlife that lives there. This method of appreciation of nature and the land is often referred to as "backyard conservation" and can be done by anyone to conserve and improve natural resources on the land and help the environment.

Backyard conservation is popular with inhabitants of cities and suburban areas. Many residents enjoy gardening, landscaping, and the pride of producing on their land, whether it is fruits and vegetables or beautiful flower gardens and landscaping. Many cities also strive to beautify the environment by creating large tracts of land devoted to parks, horticulture, and beautiful gardens.

Whether it is acres of land in the country, an average-sized suburban yard, or a tiny plot within the city, everyone can help protect the environment and beautify the surroundings. Backyard conservation provides habitat for birds and other wildlife, healthier soil, erosion control, water conservation, and nutrient management.

When trees are planted in backyards, they can provide valuable habitat for many types of wildlife. Trees can also help reduce home heating and cooling costs, help clean the air, and provide shelter from the wind. Trees in urban areas help prevent dust particles from adding to smog.

Habitat is a combination of food, water, shelter, and space that meets the needs of a species of wildlife. Even a small yard can be landscaped to attract birds, butterflies, small animals, and insects.

Amazing Plant Facts

Did you know . . . ?

- An oak tree may have more than 250,000 leaves.
- The raffia palm has the world's largest leaves—they can grow up to 65 feet (19.8 m) long.
- Ferns account for about 12,000 plant species and exist mainly in the tropics. They range in size from very small to 45 feet (13.7 m) tall.
- Island plants are naturally vulnerable because of their restricted geographic range. When tourism and other land use demands are introduced, this can easily cause a species' extinction.
- The biggest seed is on the coco-de-mar palm—a palm that only grows in the Seychelles Islands. A single seed can weigh up to 40 pounds (18.2 kg) and can take 20 years to ripen.
- Almost all cacti are restricted to the Americas. This family of succulents contains 1,650 species. They live mainly in hot, dry desert habitats.
- In developing countries, plants are the main source of medicine. Nearly 80% of the world's population relies on remedies made from plants for their principal health care.
- Rosy periwinkle is an example of how scientific investigation of a traditional remedy can promote the development of a new drug. It has been used in traditional

Trees, shrubs, and other plants provide shelter and food for wildlife. Nesting boxes, feeders, and watering sites can be added to improve the habitat.

Wildlife habitat covers the horizontal dimension (the size of the yard) as well as a vertical component from the ground to the treetops.

medicine to treat diabetes, but lab research has proved its value as a source of anticancer agents.

- Some Arctic lupine seeds were discovered in 1966 frozen in the ground in Canada. Scientists believe the seeds were at least 15,000 years old, but once the seeds thawed, some actually sprouted and grew.
- Bamboo—a huge grass with hollow, compartmentalized woody stems—provides much of the major structural materials of tropical regions, especially in Asia. Although the stems are hard and strong, they split easily. They are used to make many practical things, such as water pipes, scaffolding, posts, walls, furniture, gutters, tools, musical instruments, paper, and matting.
- Rubber *(Hevea brasiliensis)*, a native plant of the Amazon basin, is a tropical plant that produces a water-repellent, stiff, elastic latex. Natural rubber is one of the most widely used of all plant products.
- In the prehistoric forests, giant horsetails grew 150 feet (45.7 m) tall—the size of a 15-story building.
- More than 25,000 of the world's flowering plants, which is one-tenth of all the plants on Earth, are now in danger of extinction.
- A bristlecone pine tree in the White Mountains of California is around 4,700 years old.

(Sources: United Nations Environment Programme/World Conservation Monitoring Center; and Anita Ganeri, Plants, *New York: Franklin Watts, 1992)*

Planting a backyard garden is one way to learn about conservation. *(Courtesy of USDA Natural Resources Conservation Service, photo by Lynn Betts)*

Different wildlife species live in the different vertical zones, enabling several habitats to exist in a backyard setting. Trees and shrubs are also important sources of food for wildlife. Birdhouses and shelters are easy to add to a backyard habitat to increase the wildlife that visits the area. Plant species that birds enjoy can be grown to encourage wildlife visits.

Clean, fresh water is also critical in a backyard habitat. Birds, bats, butterflies, and other wildlife need a source of water. Water can be stored in a saucer, birdbath, or backyard pond.

Plants can also have practical uses in landscaping. One effective use of plants is in developing a snow fence. Living snow fences are designed plantings of trees or shrubs and native grasses located along roads or ditches, or around communities and farmsteads. These plantings create a vegetative barrier that traps and controls blowing and drifting snow.

Living snow fences are especially helpful along roads, because they can trap blowing snow and prevent snowdrifts on the road. They also help improve visibility by keeping snow from blowing across the road, as well as reduce the buildup of slush and ice on the pavement. According to the Natural Resources Conservation Service, it is estimated that a 10-foot-tall living snow fence can trap 20–30 tons of snow per linear foot.

Just as barriers of trees can prevent snow from blowing and being deposited everywhere, trees can also be planted in a row and used to block the destructive effects of the wind. These are referred to as windbreaks.

Windbreaks are linear plantings of trees and shrubs that are designed to enhance crop production, protect people and livestock, and benefit soil and water conservation. Vine and fruit tree growers, row crop farmers, livestock producers, and rural homeowners can use windbreaks.

There are many benefits to using windbreaks. They provide microclimate modification. Field and orchard windbreaks can help increase the yield of many different types of crops, especially high-value horticultural crops, such as raspberries, strawberries, and blueberries.

Tree-sheltered areas can also play a large role in animal survival. Because windbreaks can modify harsh climatic conditions, they protect newborn animals from freezing to death. Windbreaks around feedlots have been shown to improve the health and weight gain of sheep and cattle in cold climates.

According to the U.S. Department of Energy, tree-sheltered buildings, such as homes, use 10%–20% less energy for heating or cooling compared to unsheltered homes, so they also assist in energy conservation. Windbreaks made of trees and shrubs provide food and habitat for game birds and other wildlife. Windbreaks also assist in the carbon cycle. It's estimated that for each acre planted in field windbreaks, over 21 metric tons of carbon dioxide will be stored in the trees after 20 years of growth. These are just a few of the measures that can be taken to protect and conserve plant life.

CONCLUSIONS: FUTURE ISSUES AND DISCOVERIES

Food and **textile plants** didn't just happen by chance. They are the combined result of thousands of years of experimentation and research that developed from their wild ancestors. This chapter looks at the scientific advances of biotechnology, the use of seed banks, developments and experiments, plant experiments in outer space, and finally, our role in the big picture.

BIOTECHNOLOGY

Biotechnology is a general term to describe processes for using living organisms—such as plants—to create new products. It includes forms of genetic engineering, also called bioengineering or genetic modification. Genetic engineering is a quicker and more precise means of manipulating genes than traditional breeding techniques. When used with plants, it can provide a more abundant, less expensive, and more nutritious food supply.

Over centuries, humans have taken wild, naturally occurring plants and cultivated superior plants from them. For example, some food plants, such as corn, can be cultivated to give a higher yield. Other food plants, such as alfalfa, are able to produce two crops per year. Many, such as apples, have been cultivated to have higher quality fruits and seeds. Some plants have been scientifically developed to be more resistant to pests and diseases.

Breeding plants for centuries has led to a wide range of cultivated crops and plants that are raised on farms, in gardens, and in homes. The earliest farmers recognized the basics of growing better crops and began the process of cultivating and developing better plants just by selecting and planting seeds from the strongest and healthiest plants to be used as the next year's crop. Today, much research is going into the benefits of crossbreeding, cell fusion, recombinant DNA, cloning, and grafting to produce superior plants.

In recent years, science has advanced and technology has developed substantially. With the use of genetics, scientists have become more efficient at cross-fertilizing plants. Cross-fertilizing takes two parent plants, each with its own desirable characteristics. Once they've been fertilized, the resulting offspring can have the best features of each parent. This process of selection—using only the best plants—is still the most widespread method of producing new plants from old ones.

Many wild plants have been cultivated to produce other food plants that are used today. For example, the cultivation of different plant parts of the wild cabbage has produced such foods as broccoli, brussels sprouts, cabbage, and cauliflower.

Many of the grains and produce people eat today are hybrids. They're created by cross-fertilizing two related purebred parents. A major advantage of hybrids is that they are stronger and more resistant to disease and produce more food. The seeds from a hybrid plant, however, will not produce another good quality hybrid. A disadvantage to hybrids is that they require special chemical fertilization and pesticides.

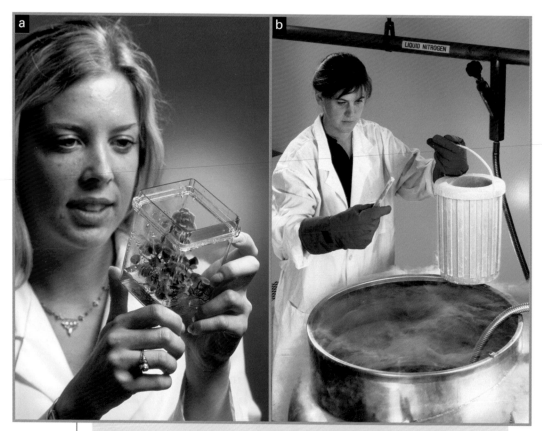

There are many lab research applications applied to plants. At left, technician Brandy Jones examines a rose plant that began as cells growing in a tissue culture. At right, plant physiologist Christina Walters lowers a container of seeds into a vat of liquid nitrogen that will cryopreserve (freeze) them. *(Photos by Scott Bauer, Courtesy of Agricultural Research Service)*

Plants are selected not only for how much they produce and how disease resistant they are, but also for things like the ability to grow in poor soil, withstand bad weather, and mature and ripen faster. Hybridization allows breeders to produce plants for particular conditions and needs.

Another scientific approach that is used to develop plants is cloning. A cutting from an adult plant is placed in a test tube containing gel growth **hormones**. From just a small amount of plant tissue, scientists are able to produce large numbers of identical plants. Scientists have been able to **clone** plants from just a single cell of the adult.

In the process of grafting, one plant is attached to, and grows on, another closely related plant. Although this technique is not new—it has been used for 2,000 years—scientists have made many advancements to make it more efficient and productive. A practical example of grafting is when a vine from a plant that consistently produces good fruit is grafted onto a parent vine—or stock vine—that is disease resistant. If the graft is successful, it will produce a plant that is disease resistant and has good fruit.

Cell fusion combines two cells of the same or different species. The downfall with this technique is that it is hard to develop a hybrid that will maintain constant traits over time. Because many genes are transferred during this process, unwanted traits may be bred into the new species.

Recombinant DNA (also known as gene-splicing) transfers small segments of DNA directly. Scientists can move genes that control specific traits into a host plant, which is then bred to produce the desired traits. A major advantage with this technique is that the specific gene carrying the desired trait can be transferred without picking up unwanted genes with undesirable traits.

As the science of genetic engineering continues to advance, larger quantities and new varieties of more nutritious foods will be developed. Future plants will become more disease- and pest-resistant. Scientific experimentation will also yield new medicines as known plants are tested and new plants are discovered.

Plant hunters are always on the lookout for undiscovered species of plants. Many of our major crops did not originate in the United States, but were brought here by immigrants. Many of these plants arrived as germplasm—seeds, cuttings, or whole plants—collected by plant collectors.

There are many benefits from collecting germplasm. New crops bred from them stand a better chance against disease and insect attack.

It also helps crops get used to new or changing growing conditions. Because of the genetic material stored in germplasm, it keeps crops healthier, more productive, and better tasting.

Early explorations have had an impact on the types of food people eat today. For example, if it had not been for earlier discoveries, there would not be food items like corn, soybeans, potatoes, berries, grapes, apples, carrots, cereal grains, onions, tomatoes, or lemons. Even the lawn grass people grow in their yards today in the United States was an immigrant to this country.

Plant exploring and collecting today is directed by the USDA's National Germplasm Resources Laboratory in Maryland. They make sure farmers have the right crops to grow enough food to feed the country. As plants continue to be collected, new germplasm is discovered, and scientists are able to find new applications for plants.

Food Products Modified by Biotechnology

Plant type	Genetic modification	Goal
Peppers, cucumbers, tomatoes	Fungal resistance	To reduce fungicide use
Coffee	Low caffeine content	To create naturally decaffeinated coffee
Tomatoes, peas, broccoli, raspberries	Controlled ripening	To lengthen shelf life and improve quality
Corn, sunflowers, soybeans	Improved nutrition	To increase the amounts of vitamins and nutrients
Tomatoes, corn, lettuce, cabbage, apples	Insect resistance	To reduce use of insecticides
Corn, peas	Controlled starch	To retain sweetness during entire shelf life
Tomatoes, corn, wheat	Herbicide tolerance	To improve weed control

(Source: USDA Agricultural Resource Service)

SEED BANKS

Because future plants have the promise of new applications and uses—such as being sources of new medicines, energy, foods, and environmental benefits—scientists keep a supply of seeds secure in seed banks. Seed banks are used to store wild plants, cultivated plants, and scientifically developed plant varieties. The seeds can either be frozen in liquid nitrogen or stored in airtight containers. Seed banks store seeds of rare plants and threatened and endangered plants for preservation. Seeds are also stored for future research. Only a small percentage of the world's plants have been tested for their potential medicinal values. Storing the seeds allows scientists to be able to study the plants in the future with new technology as it is developed. A container of seeds is lowered into a vat of liquid nitrogen that will freeze them. The vats can hold 5,000 containers of up to 2,000 seeds each. Seeds stored like this can be preserved and still germinate after thousands of years, but scientists do occasionally remove samples in order to check them and make sure they are in good condition.

DEVELOPMENTS AND EXPERIMENTS

As science and technology advance, new applications for plants are being discovered. Plants are involved in the invention of new products. For example, seedlings of guayule plants are being used in laboratory experiments to improve the plant stock. The guayule plant has shown great promise in producing experimental allergen-free latex products, such as surgical gloves. Development of these products would help thousands of people each year who are allergic to latex.

Plants are also being researched for their weed control potential. In order to protect the environment, scientists are turning to more environmentally responsible means of keeping invasive weeds from spreading. Rather than relying heavily on traditional chemical herbicides (weed killers), biocontrols are being developed. For example, if the pathogens that destroy a weed can be identified by studying the actual weed, then the weed can be selectively destroyed without harming any of the other types of plants or soil around it.

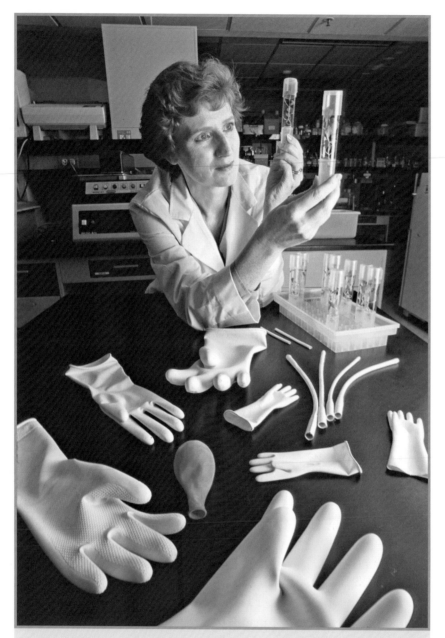

In her laboratory, plant physiologist Katrina Cornish checks seedlings produced for use in experiments to improve guayule plants. The experimental, allergen-free latex products shown were made from guayule. *(Photo by Jack Dykinga. Courtesy of USDA Agricultural Research Service)*

Scientists are also looking at the role of plants in controlling erosion. This is especially important in areas that receive excessive amounts of wind and in fragile areas such as desert ecosystems that suffer great damage from erosion. If plants can bind the soil, making it more stable, precious soil resources can be conserved. Through the use of a wind tunnel, scientists can determine how live plants and straw residue slow windblown soil erosion.

As a food source, flowers are studied in laboratories in order to discover future potential. For example, sunflowers produce oil used in cooking.

Plants are an important food source for animals. As new plants are discovered and developed, they not only benefit us directly, but they also benefit livestock. Some scientists extract chemicals to determine which plants are safe, palatable, and nutritious for livestock.

Plants are also a promising source of future energy. Although the United States has only 5% of the world's population, it accounts for a quarter of the world's energy demand and usage. Many scientists are turning to plants to supply environmentally friendlier energy resources.

Biomass feedstocks can be used to manufacture all of the fuels and chemicals currently being manufactured from traditional fossil fuels like oil and gas. Feedstock is any organic matter that is available on a renewable basis for conversion to energy. Feedstocks include wood, sawdust, bark, wood edgings, farm animal wastes, the organic portion of municipal solid waste, sewage, and some types of industrial wastes.

Biomass fuels—or biofuels—are solid, liquid, or gas fuels derived from feedstock. For example, there is landfill-to-gas methane, ethanol-blend gasoline from corn, or biodiesel auto fuel from soybeans. Today, some cars run on alcohol made from sugarcane. In areas of Malaysia, special varieties of palm trees are being cultivated. The palm tree oil is blended with diesel after processing.

Unlike fossil fuels—which take millions of years to form—waste biomass is an energy source that may help solve our environmental

Scientists are always looking to the future for new discoveries and developments. (a) A scientist examines the roots of a leafy spurge from Russia for pathogens which could be used for biocontrol of this weed in the United States. (b) A technician measures a plant's role in slowing erosion. (c) A geneticist (left) and technician pollinate sunflowers to develop new inbred lines that produce oil. (d) A chemist extracts chemicals to determine which plants are safe, palatable, and nutritious for livestock. *(a, photo by Keith Weller, courtesy of Agricultural Research Service; b, d, photos by Scott Bauer, courtesy of Agricultural Research Service; c, photo by Russ Hanson, courtesy of Agricultural Research Service)*

hazardous wastes and recycling problems. Plants are also being used to study the ecological conditions of our environment. They may be able to measure and help manage against environmental pollution. For example, lichens are extremely sensitive to air pollution—specifically sulfur dioxide. If lichens are not growing naturally around cities, that is a good indicator that high pollution levels exist. Water pollution can also be detected and studied. In water areas where an excessive amount of blue-green algae (cyanobacteria) is growing, this is a good indicator of water pollution. These unique abilities of plants and plantlike organisms can enable us to be more environmentally knowledgeable in the future.

PLANTS IN SPACE

Plants may seem like something that would only be found on Earth, but that's not the case. Today, scientists who are living and working on the International Space Station are studying plants and the effects that outer space has on them.

In order for space exploration to be feasible, astronauts have to have a way to feed themselves—especially if they spend months in space. They also have to make sure that their limited resources, such as oxygen, water, and soil, are preserved and well managed. These issues are critical to their survival.

Space agricultural research also affects agriculture on Earth because it has the potential to improve the ways farmers grow and process foods here. According to the U.S. Department of Agriculture, some of the space-based research currently being conducted includes the following:

- Testing new ways to package and preserve food for future space missions, as well as for food on Earth
- Exploring ways to use space technology in order to more effectively fertilize plants on Earth
- Developing technologies to efficiently use and recycle water
- Planting specialized crops that can grow in microgravity

If astronauts can learn to grow, harvest, and store food in space, this will allow them to explore planets like Mars and places even farther away—places that would require them to be away from Earth for months or years. Astronauts are experimenting with new ways to grow seeds, conserve soil resources, and even work with new kinds of food. Space agriculture also presents extraordinary possibilities for increasing crop yield—discoveries that will help people everywhere.

Plant research in space is not a new concept. Research began during the early days of space exploration. For example, the Apollo astronauts who landed on the Moon brought lunar soil back to Earth, where scientists attempted to grow seeds in it. As space exploration has become more advanced and sophisticated, so has plant research. The National Aeronautic and Space Administration (NASA) is interested in creating bioregenerative life support systems that can support human and plant life forever.

Bioregenerative life support systems perform all the basic functions of a life support system. Its natural cycle allows it to continue regenerating itself. Earth is a perfect example of a regenerative system with natural cycles. Earth continually provides food, water, and air. In space, plants provide food, carbon dioxide uptake, oxygen generation, and water purification.

There are several challenges for space-based plants, however. The lack of gravity in outer space presents some unique dilemmas, because it is the gravity on Earth that helps plants establish strong rooting. Available sunlight and nutrients are other issues, as are insects for cross-pollination, a controlled climate, and the availability of clean water.

Plants and people work well together in a closed system like this, however. Humans breathe air and produce carbon dioxide—plants consume the carbon dioxide and give off oxygen.

On Earth, energy is in the form of sunlight, but in space, availability of sunlight is not constant like it is on Earth. In space, the source of energy is provided in the form of artificial light. Specifically, the same Light Emitting Diodes (LEDs) that are used on Earth in many electronics. LEDs are used because they give light in the specific frequencies that plants need in order for photosynthesis to take place. LEDs are also more energy efficient that other light sources.

Clean water is created from the self-sustaining, natural cleaning and filtration systems that are created in the space-life support systems. Gravity is generated through microgravity systems developed for long-term trips.

Space-based research is already helping Earth-based agriculture. Studies are being conducted involving custom crops that withstand hostile conditions, resist disease, and require less space to grow in.

Scientists believe that if food production can be sustained in space, then it will be possible for human life to be established anywhere in the universe. For space exploration involving many months, the best system for growing crops is with Controlled Environment Agriculture (CEA). Plants are grown in growth chambers controlled by computers, where all the environmental factors can be controlled, such as nutrients, light, humidity, and temperature. A favored growth method is *hydroponics*. This has another advantage: Water transpired by the plants can be collected and used as drinking water by the astronauts.

Research is also being conducted on controlling the greenhouse environment to the point that light and nutrients are supplied at specific times when optimal conditions in the plants themselves exist. Some day, scientists plan to have space agriculture operated by automated or robotic crop production systems.

One thing scientists have discovered is that plants grown in a controlled environment usually produce more food than plants grown in the field. This is because a controlled environment is a less stressful environment for plants—temperature, humidity, light, water, and nutrients are all tailored to plants' individual needs.

Special seeds—called super-dwarf seeds—have also been developed for use in outer space. Different varieties have been developed, such as wheat, rice, tomatoes, soybeans, peas, and peppers. These crops are genetically engineered to only grow to short heights so that they can be grown on shelves. One version of the wheat—called apogee wheat—developed by researchers at Utah State University, took a decade to develop and is half the height of normal wheat. It grows about 12 inches (30.5 cm) tall. It has fewer branches and smaller leaves than normal wheat. The plants also grow closer together. Super-dwarf seeds produce high yields (up to three times higher), which also makes them an attractive solution to growing food in space.

Plants may also have a future place on Mars. Researchers have developed a genetically altered mustard plant that glows when it is stressed. Scientists see testing this plant as the first step toward human colonization of Mars. Scientists at the University of Florida were able to splice a fluorescent gene from a jellyfish into a mustard plant. They believe adverse conditions—such as disease or lack of water—will trigger the plant to glow. By studying these effects, it may be possible to discover how to sustain plant, then human life, on Mars. Researchers want NASA to test the fluorescent plants on a mission to Mars in 2007. One version of the plant will glow green in soil that contains heavy metals. Another will glow blue if the soil contains too much peroxide. Earth scientists will be able to monitor the plants' reactions to these conditions via camera images.

OUR ROLE IN THE BIG PICTURE

As we have seen in this volume, plants play a critical role in our lives every day—such as in the food we eat, the air we breathe, shelter, health care, and clothing. There are many things humans can do to help now and in the future. For example, they can plant natural vegetation in their backyards. They can also be careful not to rely heavily on chemical fertilizers and herbicides.

Many areas that have important plants are being protected by being made into national parks and reserves. This not only protects the plants but also the rest of the ecosystem.

Erosion can be controlled through the use of plants in the Southwest. Many organizations—both government and private—have been developed in the last few years. The goal of these organizations is to educate the public about the natural resources people may take for granted, how to protect them, and how to ensure their existence and survival in the future.

In areas where vegetation has been destroyed—by flooding, mudslides, earthquakes, drought, or fire—people can replant the bare ground. This process of reclamation not only helps the ecosystem, it also controls erosion and discourages invasive species from taking a strong hold in the ecosystem.

The passing of laws by governments can also be effective in halting the damage being done to plant life. For example, strictly enforced air quality requirements, laws controlling clear-cutting of forests, and the creation of responsible long-term land use guidelines are critical to the health and future of plants.

There are many ways to become involved by checking into local, state, and national environmental organizations. These are good places to gain valuable information on conservation and good land stewardship practices. It's up to each one of us to do our share so that those in the future will benefit.

The Divisions of the Plant Kingdom

Type of Plant	Division	Common Name
Nonvascular	Bryophyta	mosses
	Hepatophyta	liverworts
	Anthocerotophyta	hornworts
	Chlorophyta	green algae
Vascular, seedless	Psilophyta	whisk ferns
	Lycopodiophyta	club mosses
	Equisetophyta	horsetails
	Pteridophyta	ferns
Vascular, seeds		
Gymnosperms	Cycadophyta	cycads
	Ginkgophyta	ginkgoes
	Coniferophyta	conifers
	Gnetophyta	gnetophytes
Angiosperms	Magnoliophyta	flowering plants

Flowering Plants

Flowering plants (Magnoliophyta) is the largest group of plants, with about 250,000 different species. These species have been classified into families. There are more than 300 families of flowering plants. The following table illustrates some of the most common families.

Major Family	Common Members
Gramineae (grass family)	Pampas grass, barley, bluegrass, corn, bamboo, millet, oats, rye, sugarcane, wheat, rice
Leguminosae (legume family)	Wisteria, pea, peanut, soybean, sweet pea, clover, bean, alfalfa, acacia
Orchidaceae (orchid family)	Orchids
Rosaceae (rose family)	Rose, strawberry, plum, raspberry, pear, cherry, blackberry, apple
Aceraceae (maple family)	Maple, sycamore, box elder, hornbeam
Cactaceae (cactus family)	Cactus, opuntia
Liliaceae (lily family)	Lily, amaryllis, aloe, asparagus, garlic, hyacinth, onion, tulip, violet
Arecaceae (palm family)	Coconut palm, date palm
Cruciferae (cabbage family)	Cabbage, broccoli, cauliflower, radish, turnip, watercress
Solanaceae (potato family)	Potato, petunia, eggplant, thorn apple, tobacco, tomato
Umbelliferae (carrot family)	Carrot, celery, caraway, anise, parsnip, parsley

GLOSSARY

abscisic acid   A hormone produced in plants that usually inhibits growth and germination of seeds; also causes guard cells to take up water and swell, thereby closing leaf stomata.

acid rain   Rain that is made abnormally acidic by gases released from the burning of fuels like coal; gases dissolve in the water in the air and fall as acid rain, snow, or mist.

adaptation   A structure or behavior that helps an organism survive in its environment.

aerial roots   Roots that absorb water from the air.

alcohol   A liquid produced from sugar that may be used as a fuel.

algae   Plant or plantlike organisms that are chiefly aquatic; they usually contain chlorophyll but lack stems, roots, and leaves.

angiosperm   Plant that reproduces by means of flowers and whose seeds are enclosed in fruits.

annual   A plant that completes its life cycle in a single year.

anther   The male part of a flower, which produces pollen.

antheridium   The male reproductive organ of lower plants.

aquatic   An organism that lives in water.

archegonium   The female reproductive organ of lower plants.

asexual reproduction   Production of new plants not involving reproductive cells, or *gametes*; includes binary fission, vegetative propagation.

auxin   A growth regulator, or hormone, that stimulates cell elongation and division, promoting growth and development.

axillary buds   Lateral buds situated at the junction of a leaf stalk and stem.

bacteria   Extremely small living things that bring about the decay of plant and animal remains and wastes.

bark   The outer layer of a woody stem such as a tree, made up of layers of dead cells.

binary fission   A method of asexual reproduction among some single-celled organisms involving division of the cell into two identical daughter cells.

biome   A major area of the world with its special kind of climate, plants, and animals.

bog   A wet, spongy marsh area.

botanist   A person trained in the study of plant life.

botany   The branch of biology dealing with plant life.

bract   A leaf on a flower stalk specialized to protect a flower.

bulb   An underground part of a plant that stores food in its leaves.

cambium   The layer of a tree's trunk and branches located between the xylem and the phloem.

carbon dioxide   A colorless gas that makes up 0.03% of the atmosphere; released through the respiration of living things.

carnivore   An animal or plant that feeds on flesh.

carpel   The female seed-bearing organ of a flowering plant, which contains the stigma (on a stalk or style) and the ovary.

cell   The basic structural unit of plants and animals; a plant cell is surrounded by a nonliving cell wall.

cellulose   The material of which plant walls are composed.

cereals   Grasses that produce an edible grain.

chlorophyll   A green pigment that occurs chiefly in palisade cells of leaves and that is required in the food-making process, photosynthesis.

chloroplast   The body within the plant cell that contains chlorophyll.

clone   A group of organisms descended asexually from a common ancestor.

community   A population of plants and animals that live together and affect each other.

coniferous   Trees that bear seeds in cones made of overlapping scales; coniferous trees, which are gymnosperms, include pines, spruces, and firs.

corm   A short underground stem that stores food and reproduces the plant.

cotyledon   A specialized, food-storing leaf within a seed.

cuticle   A waxy substance secreted by epidermal cells on their outer walls.

cutting   A cutoff part of a plant from which a new plant is grown.

decay (decaying)   To rot as a result of the action of bacteria or fungi.

deciduous trees   Trees that shed their leaves each year at the end of the growing season.

deserts   Those regions where there is little rainfall and where few plants and animals live.

disperse   To spread spores or seeds away from the parent plant to prevent overcrowding.

dominant   Most important; the plant or animal species that largely determines what other species share its habitat is said to be dominant.

dormant period   A time during which a plant rests and makes little or no new growth.

ecology   The study of how living things affect, and are affected by, their environment.

egg   Female reproductive cell with its own provision of food for the growing embryo; the male *sperm* must fertilize the egg before development of the embryo can begin.

embryo   A young plant in its seed, before the beginning of its rapid growth; each embryo within its seed has the beginnings of its first leaves, first root, and first bud.

endangered   Close to extinction.

endosperm   Food storage tissue that surrounds the embryo plant in a seed of a flowering plant.

environment   The world around us, or our surroundings, including all living things; the place where an animal or plant lives may be called its environment.

enzymes   Chemicals made by the cell that speed up the rate of chemical reactions inside the cell.

epidermal   Having to do with the epidermis.

epidermis   The protective outermost layer of a plant cell.

erosion   The wearing away of the land surface.

ethylene   A colorless gas that functions as a hormone in plants, causing fruit to ripen, petals to droop, and leaves to fall.

evaporation   The change of a liquid into a vapor.

evergreen   A plant that is green year-round and that does not lose all its leaves in winter, such as a pine tree.

evolve   The changes in a species over long periods that give rise to a new species.

extinct   No longer in existence.

fern   A flowerless plant that has leaves with veins.

fertilization   The fusion of a male sex cell with a female sex cell.

fibrous roots   A root that branches in all directions, such as with grass.

flaccid   Describes a plant cell that is wilting because of lack of water; flaccid cells give no support to a plant, which becomes limp.

flagella   Tail-like structures of certain one-celled organisms.

flower   The reproductive organ of the angiosperms, usually consisting of petals, sepals, stamens, and a pistil.

food chain   A chain of living things through which energy is passed as food.

fossil   The preserved record of an organism that lived long ago.

fossil fuels   Those fuels (oil, gas, and coal) that have been formed in the ground over millions of years from the decay of living things.

frond   The leaflike structure of large algae such as seaweeds or the usually finely divided leaves of ferns.

fruit   A matured ovary, or a cluster of matured ovaries, usually containing one or more seeds.

fungi   Organisms that do not carry out photosynthesis but must take their food from living or dead plants and animals.

gamete   A reproductive cell such as a sperm or egg; sexual reproduction involves fertilization, which involves the fusion of male and female gametes.

gametophyte   A stage in the life cycle of plants, which produces gametes.

geotropism   Plant growth in response to the force of gravity; gravitropism

germination   The sprouting or resumption of growth by a seed, spore, or other reproductive structure.

gibberellin   A substance produced by plants that stimulates stem and root growth, seed germination, and flowering.

global warming   The process by which Earth is getting warmer because of changes in the atmosphere caused by human actions.

glucose   A type of sugar that is used by cells for energy.

grains   Grasses that are annuals and are grown as crops.

gravitropism   Bending in response to gravity; also called *geotropism*.

gravity   A force that pulls objects toward Earth.

greenhouse effect   The warming of the surface and lower atmosphere of Earth, which is compounded by gases in the atmosphere, such as the carbon dioxide emitted from burning fossil fuels.

guard cells   Pairs of epidermal cells that enclose and regulate the size of openings called *stomata*.

gymnosperm   A woody, seed-bearing plant whose seeds are not enclosed in ovaries; they include the ginkgo, cycads, and such conifers as pines and junipers.

habitat   A place with a particular environment where plants and animals live.

heartwood   The dead, woody vessels in the center of a tree.

herbicide   A poison used to kill unwanted plants and weeds.

herbivores   Animals that eat plants.

hormone   A substance produced by living organisms that regulates growth and development.

host plant   A plant from which another plant steals nutrients.

hybrid   The result of crossbreeding two plants that are not alike.

hyphae   The individual threadlike part of the body of a fungus.

inflorescence   A group of flowers on a single main stem.

leaves   Lateral outgrowths from plant stems, which function primarily in food manufacture by photosynthesis.

lenticels   Tiny holes in the bark of a tree that allow gases in and out for respiration.

lichen   A type of plant consisting of an alga living within a fungus.

lignin   A complex compound that is a vital part of wood; lignin functions as a binder and support for the fibers of many plants.

liverwort   A flowerless plant without veins and with a life cycle in which a spore-producing phase alternates with a dominant gamete-producing phase.

meristem   A plant tissue composed of cells that are capable of frequent division; meristem tissue is found near the tips of roots and stems and, in many plants, as an inner layer (called *cambium*) along the lengths of roots and stems.

mesophyll   The name given to the palisade and spongy layers of a leaf.

metabolism   The chemical processes in cells that are essential to life.

micropyle   The tiny hole in the ovule through which the pollen tube enters during fertilization.

minerals   Any of certain elements, such as iron, that are needed by plants and animals.

molecule   The smallest particle of a substance that retains all the properties of that substance.

monocarpic   Flowering once and then dying.

moss   A flowerless plant that reproduces by spores.

nectar   A sugary liquid produced by some flowers to attract insects.

niche   The position that an animal or plant holds in the community.

node   The region of a stem where a leaf or secondary branch grows.

nucleus   The control center of a cell.

nutrients   Substances that plants and animals need in order to grow.

organ   Major part of a plant that has a specific job; for instance, a leaf, stem, or root.

organism   Any living being.

osmosis   The movement of water molecules through a membrane from a weak to a strong solution.

ovary   The enlarged base of a flower's pistil in which ovules develop.

ovule   An immature seed, containing an egg nucleus, that develops after fertilization into a seed that contains an embryo plant.

ovum   An unfertilized egg.

oxygen   The gas that makes up nearly 21% of the air; it is essential for life.

palisade cell   A long, cylindrical leaf cell that contains chlorophyll and in which most food making occurs.

parasite   An organism that lives in or on another organism.

peat   Partially carbonized vegetable tissue formed by partial decomposition in water of various plants.

penicillin   A medicine used to treat infectious diseases; it was developed from mold.

perennial   A plant that grows for more than two years.

pesticides   Chemicals used to kill pests such as insects and rodents.

phloem   The plant food-conducting tissue that consists mostly of sieve tube cells.

photosynthesis   The manufacture of food, mainly sugar, from carbon dioxide and water in the presence of chlorophyll, using solar energy and releasing oxygen.

phototropism   Growth induced by the stimulus of light; growth can be either away from light (negative phototropism) or toward light (positive phototropism).

pigment   A substance that produces colors in plant or animal tissues; plant pigments include chlorophylls (greens), anthocyanins (reds, purples, blues), and carotenoids (yellows, oranges, orange-reds).

pistil   The central structure of a flower that encloses one or more ovules.

plumule   The first shoot that grows from a seed.

pollen   The male sex cells of seed plants.

pollen tube   An outgrowth of a pollen grain carrying male sex cells to the egg in the ovule.

pollination   In angiosperms, the transfer of pollen from a stamen to a stigma.

pollution   The release of substances into the air, water, or land that may upset the natural balance of the environment; such substances are called *pollutants.*

pore   A very small hole.

protein   The complex chemicals necessary for an organism to grow.

radicle   The first root that grows from a seed.

rain forest   A dense forest found in the hot, tropical areas of the world.

reproduction   Process by which a new organism is produced by one or a pair of parent organisms of the same kind.

respiration   The chemical process by which organic material is broken down, releasing energy.

rhizome   An underground stem that grows horizontally and is often enlarged with stored food.

roots   Parts of a plant that take in water, usually from the soil.

sap   The juice, made up of water, sugars, and minerals inside the stem of a plant.

sapling   A young tree or shrub.

sapwood   The younger outer layer of a woody stem.

seed   A seed contains a tiny plant and a store of food before it begins to grow.

seedling   A very young plant grown from a seed.

self-pollination   The transfer of male pollen to a female stigma in the same flower or in a separate flower on the same plant; self-pollination tends to produce weak plants after a few generations.

sexual reproduction   Production of new plants by the fusion of male and female gametes, either sperm and egg, or pollen grain and egg, within an ovule.

sieve tube   A series of sieve-like cells joined end to end; they are passageways for food in the form of sugary sap.

skototropism   Growth toward darkness.

species   Group of organisms that are alike, apart from minor variations.

sperm   The male reproductive cell that fertilizes a female egg.

spores   The reproductive structures of ferns and mosses.

sporophyte   A stage in the life cycle of plants that produce spores.

stamen   The male pollen-producing structure of a flower.

starch   The form in which plants store excess food; a starch molecule is made up of hundreds of molecules of glucose.

statolith   A movable starch grain that occurs in some plant cells and that moves in response to gravity, stimulating vertical growth when a plant part is tipped from its normal position.

stem   The part of a plant from which the leaves and flowers grow.

stigma   The part of a flower's pistil, usually located at its top, on which pollen must be deposited for pollination to occur.

stimulus   A change in the environment that can be detected by an organism.

stoma (pl., stomata)   An opening between two guard cells in the epidermis of a plant; guard cells regulate the size of stomata, which are passageways for the exchange of gases between plants and the atmosphere.

succession   Changes that cause one community to be replaced by another.

succulent   A plant that has thick fleshy tissues, such as stems and leaves that can store water.

symbiosis   The relationship of two or more organisms that live closely together to the benefit of both.

taproot   A large main root of some plants.

tendril   A slender, coiling structure that aids the support of plant stems; it is usually a modified steam or leaf.

terminal bud   The bud at the top of a shoot from which the main growth of a plant continues.

textile plant   A plant with fibers that are woven into materials called textiles.

topiary   The art of training, cutting, and trimming trees or shrubs into ornamental shapes.

tracheid cell   An elongated cell with thick, pitted walls through which water and minerals are conducted.

transpiration   The emission of water vapor from plants, chiefly from leaf stomata.

tropism   A growth response resulting from an external stimulus, such as light, darkness, gravity, or touch.

tuber   An underground stem or root swollen with food, such as a potato.

turgor pressure   The pressure that develops in a cell as a result of the uptake of water; the pressure is exerted against the cell wall.

ultraviolet (UV) light   Light that is not visible to the human eye but which is produced in large amounts by the sun.

vacuole   A space within a cell, enclosed by a membrane and containing a water solution of sugars and other substances.

vascular plant   A plant with a system of tubes that carry water and food throughout the plant.

vegetative reproduction   Plant reproduction by a vegetative part of a plant—such as a leaf, root, or stem cutting—that does not involve fusion of sex cells.

vessel cells   Elongated cells that are joined end to end, forming hollow tubes that conduct water and minerals.

water table   The natural level of water in the soil; in dry places, it may be down very deep.

wetland   Land or areas that are covered often intermittently with shallow water or saturated water.

xylem   A complex plant tissue—composed of such cells as tracheid, vessel, and ray cells, and wood fibers—which functions mainly to conduct water and minerals.

BOOKS

Alderton, David. *Plants.* New York: Ladybird Books, 1997.

Aldis, Rodney. *Rain Forests.* New York: Dillon Press, 1991.

Alexander, Taylor R., Will Burnett, and Herbert Zim. *Botany: A Golden Science Guide.* Racine, Wis.: Western Publishing Company Inc., 1970.

Allan, Mea. *Darwin and His Flowers: The Key to Natural Selection.* New York: Taplinger Publishing Co. Inc., 1977.

Allen, Missy. *Dangerous Flora.* Encyclopedia of Danger. Broomall, Pa.: Chelsea House, 1993.

Amsel, Sheri. *A Wetland Walk.* Brookfield, Conn.: Millbrook Press Inc., 1993.

Asimov, Isaac. *How Did We Find Out About Photosynthesis?* New York: Walker and Company, 1989.

Bates, Jeffrey. *Seeds to Plants: Projects with Botany.* New York: Franklin Watts, 1991.

Behme, Robert L. *Incredible Plants: Oddities, Curiosities & Eccentricities.* New York: Sterling, 1992.

Bender, Lionel. *Plant.* Eyewitness Guide. New York: Alfred A. Knopf, 1989.

Bender, Lionel. *Plants.* New York: Gloucester Press, 1988.

Bender, Lionel. *Tree.* Eyewitness Guide. New York: Alfred A. Knopf, 1988.

Brown, Anne Ensign. *Monarchs of the Forest: The Story of the Redwoods.* New York: Dodd, Mead, 1984.

Burnie, David. *Plant.* Eyewitness Books. New York: Alfred A. Knopf, 1989.

Burnie, David. *Tree.* New York: Alfred A. Knopf, 1988.

Carolin, Roger. *Incredible Plants.* San Francisco: Weldon Owen Inc., 1997.

Catherall, Ed. *Exploring Plants.* Chatham, N.J.: Raintree Steck-Vaughn Publications, 1989.

Cochrane, Jennifer. *Plant Ecology.* New York: The Bookwright Press, 1987.

Coil, Suzanne M. *Poisonous Plants.* New York: Franklin Watts, 1991.

Collinson, Alan. *Grasslands.* Ecology Watch. New York: Macmillan Children's Group, 1992.

Cronk, Q., and J. Fuller. *Plant Invaders: The Threat to Natural Ecosystems.* New York: Chapman & Hall, 1995.

Dowden, Anne Ophelia. *From Flower to Fruit.* New York: Crowell, 1984.

Duddington, C.L. *Evolution and Design in the Plant Kingdom.* New York: Thomas Y. Crowell Company, 1969.

Dunphy, Madeleine. *Here Is the Wetland.* New York: Hyperion Books for Children, 1996.

Fischer-Nagel, Heiderose and Andreas. *Fir Trees.* New York: Carolrhoda Books, 1989.

Fleisher, Paul. *Mountain Stream.* Tarrytown, N.Y.: Marshall Cavendish Corporation, 1998.

Fleisher, Paul. *Pond.* Tarrytown, N.Y.: Marshall Cavendish Corporation, 1998.

Fowler, Allan. *All Along the River.* Danbury, Conn.: Franklin Watts, 1998.

Fowler, Allan. *Life in a Pond.* Danbury, Conn.: Franklin Watts, 1998.

Fowler, Allan. *Life in a Wetland.* Danbury, Conn.: Franklin Watts, 1998.

Fowler, Allan. *Our Living Forests.* Danbury, Conn.: Children's Press, 1999.

Galston, Arthur. *Green Wisdom: The Inside Story of Plant Life.* New York: Basic Books Inc., 1981.

Galston, Arthur, Peter Davies, and Ruth Sattler. *The Life of the Green Plant.* 3rd ed. Englewood Cliffs, N.J.: Prentice-Hall Inc., 1980.

Ganeri, Anita. *Plants.* New York: Franklin Watts, 1992.

Ganeri, Anita. *Plant Science.* New York: Dillon Press, 1993.

Ganeri, Anita. *What's Inside Plants?* New York: Peter Bedrick Books, 1993.

Gibbons, Gail. *Marshes & Swamps.* New York: Holiday House Inc., 1998.

Giesecke, Ernestine. *Desert Plants.* Des Plaines, Ill.: Reed Educational & Professional Publishing, 1999.

Giesecke, Ernestine. *Forest Plants.* Des Plaines, Ill.: Reed Educational & Professional Publishing, 1999.

Giesecke, Ernestine. *Pond Plants.* Des Plaines, Ill.: Reed Educational & Professional Publishing, 1999.

Giesecke, Ernestine. *River Plants.* Des Plaines, Ill.: Reed Educational & Professional Publishing, 1999.

Giesecke, Ernestine. *Seashore Plants.* Des Plaines, Ill.: Reed Educational & Professional Publishing, 1999.

Giesecke, Ernestine. *Wetland Plants.* Des Plaines, Ill.: Reed Educational & Professional Publishing, 1999.

Goldish, Meish. *How Plants Get Food.* Chatham, N.J.: Raintree Steck-Vaughn Publications, 1989.

Greenaway, Theresa. *Cycles in Nature: Plant Life.* New York: Raintree Steck-Vaughn Publishers, 2001.

Greenaway, Theresa. *Ferns.* Madison, N.J.: Raintree Steck-Vaughn, 1992.

Greenaway, Theresa. *Fir Trees.* Madison, N.J.: Raintree Steck-Vaughn, 1990.

Greenaway, Theresa. *Mosses & Liverworts.* Madison, N.J.: Raintree Steck-Vaughn, 1992.

Greenaway, Theresa. *Woodland Trees.* Madison, N.J.: Raintree Steck-Vaughn, 1990.

Greene, Carol. *Caring for Our Forests.* Springfield, N.J.: Enslow Publishers Inc. 1991.

Harlow, Rosie, and Gareth Morgan. *Trees & Leaves.* New York: Franklin Watts, 1991.

Hester, Nigel. *The Living Pond.* Danbury, Conn.: Franklin Watts, 1990.

Hester, Nigel. *The Living Seashore.* Danbury, Conn.: Franklin Watts, 1992.

Hufford, Terry L. *Botany: Basic Concepts in Plant Biology.* New York: Harper & Row, 1978.

Hunt, Francis P. *Discovering Plant Life.* London: Sceptre Books Ltd., 1983.

James. L., J. Evans, M. Ralphs, and R. Child, eds. *Noxious Range Weeds.* Builder, Colo.: Westview Press, 1991.

Johnson, Sylvia. *Mosses.* Minneapolis, Minn.: Lerner, 1983.

Julivert, Angels. *The Life of Plants.* Invisible World. Broomall, Pa.: Chelsea House, 1994.

Kerrod, Robin. *Plant Life.* Tarrytown, N.Y.: Marshall Cavendish, 1994.

Kite, L. Patricia. *Insect-Eating Plants.* Brookfield, Conn.: Millbrook Press Inc. 1995.

Klein, Richard. *The Green World: An Introduction to Plants and People.* New York: Harper & Row Publishers, 1978.

Knapp, Brian. *Visual Science Encyclopedia: Plants.* Danbury, Conn.: Grolier Educational, 2002.

Krupinski, Loretta. *Into the Woods: A Woodland Scrapbook.* New York: HarperCollins Children's Books, 1997.

Lambert, Mark. *Plant Life.* Danbury, Conn.: Franklin Watts, 1983.

Landau, Elaine. *Endangered Plants.* New York: A First Book, 1992.

Leggett, Jeremy. *Dying Forests.* North Bellmore, N.J.: Marshall Cavendish, 1991.

Lerner, Carol. *Cactus.* New York: Morrow Junior Books, 1992.

Lerner, Carol. *Pitcher Plants: The Elegant Insect Traps.* New York: William Morrow, 1983.

Lerner, Carol. *Plant Families.* New York: William Morrow, 1989.

Llamas, Andreu. *The Mysterious Jungles.* Invisible World of Plants. Broomall, Pa.: Chelsea House, 1996.

Llamas, Andreu. *Plants of the Desert.* Broomall, Pa.: Chelsea House Publishers, 1996.

Llamas, Andreu. *Plants of the Forest.* Broomall, Pa.: Chelsea House Publishers, 1995.

Llamas, Andreu. *The Vegetation of Rivers, Lakes, and Swamps.* Broomall, Pa.: Chelsea House Publishers, 1996.

Madgwick, Wendy. *Cacti & Other Succulents.* Madison, N.J.: Raintree Steck-Vaughn, 1992.

Madgwick, Wendy. *Flowering Plants.* Madison, N.J.: Raintree Steck-Vaughn, 1990.

Marcus, Elizabeth. *Amazing World of Plants.* Mahwah, N.J.: Troll Associates, 1984.

Marshall, David, and Jane Walker. *The Seashore.* Brookfield, Conn.: Millbrook Press Inc., 1995.

Morgan, Nina. *The Plant Cycle.* New York: Thomson Learning, 1993.

Morris, Neil. *Rivers & Lakes.* New York: Crabtree Publishing Company, 1998.

Morris, Ting, and Neil Morris. *Growing Things.* New York: Franklin Watts, 1994.

Murray, Peter. *Deserts.* Chanhassen, Minn.: Child's World Inc., 1997.

Myers, Norman. *A Wealth of Wild Species: Storehouse for Human Welfare.* Boulder, Colo.: Westview Press Inc., 1983.

Nations, James D. *Tropical Rain Forests: Endangered Environments.* New York: Franklin Watts, 1988.

Nielsen, Nancy J. *Carnivorous Plants.* New York: Franklin Watts, 1992.

O'Mara, Anna. *Deserts.* Danbury, Conn.: Children's Press, 1996.

Overbeck, Cynthia. *Cactus.* Chicago: Lerner Publications, 1982.

Parker, Jane, and Steve Parker. *Deserts.* Danbury, Conn.: Franklin Watts, 1998.

Patent, Dorothy Hinshaw. *Flowers for Everyone.* New York: Cobblehill, 1990.

Penny, Malcolm. *How Plants Grow.* New York: Benchmark Books, 1997.

Platt, Richard. *Plants Bite Back!* New York: DK Publishing, 1999.

Pluckrose, Henry. *Flowers.* Danbury, Conn.: Children's Press, 1994.

Pluckrose, Henry. *Seashore.* Danbury, Conn.: Children's Press, 1994.

Pope, Joyce. *Plants and Flowers.* Mahwah, N.J.: Troll Associates, 1993.

Pope, Joyce. *Plant Partnerships.* New York: Facts On File, 1991.

Prevost, John F. *Orchids.* Minneapolis, Minn.: ABDO Publishing Company, 1996.

Pringle, Laurence. *Being a Plant.* New York: Thomas Y. Crowell, 1983.

Rahn, Joan E. *Plants Up Close.* Boston: Houghton Mifflin, 1981.

Ricciuti, Edward R. *Plants in Danger.* New York: HarperCollins Children's Books, 1979.

Royston, Angela. *Strange Plants.* Des Plaines, Ill.: Reed Educational & Professional Publishing, 1999.

Sabin, Louis. *Plants, Seeds and Flowers.* Mahwah, N.J.: Troll Associates, 1985.

Silver, Donald M. *One Small Square: Seashore.* New York: W.H. Freeman & Company, 1993.

Silverstein, Alvin. *Monerans and Protists*. Taxonomy. New York: 21st Century Books, 1996.

Staub, Frank. *America's Wetlands.* Minneapolis, Minn.: Lerner Publishing Group, 1994.

Stefoff, Rebecca. *Flytrap.* Tarrytown, N.Y.: Marshall Cavendish, 1998.

Stone, Lynn M. *Wetlands.* Vero Beach, Fla.: Rourke Corporation, 1996.

Taylor, Barbara. *Incredible Plants.* London: Dorling Kindersley Limited, 1997.

Tesar, Jenny. *Endangered Habitats.* New York: Facts On File, 1991.

Tesar, Jenny. *Green Plants.* Woodbridge, Conn.: Blackbirch Press Inc., 1993.

Tesar, Jenny. *Shrinking Forests.* New York: Facts On File, 1991.

Warburton, Lois. *Rain Forests.* New York: Facts On File, 1991.

Westbrooks, R. *Invasive Plants, Changing the Landscape of America: Fact Book.* Federal Interagency Committee for the Management of Noxious and Exotic Weeds (FICMNEW). Washington, D.C.: 1998.

Wexler, Jerome. *Flowers, Fruits, Seeds.* Englewood Cliffs, N. J.: Prentice Hall, 1987.

Williams, Brian. *The Living World.* Visual Factfinder. New York: Kingfisher Books, 1993.

JOURNALS

Armstrong, W.P. "Devil's Claws." *Pacific Horticulture*, 53: 19-23.

Cook, Robert. "Attractions of the Flesh." *Natural History*, January 1982, pp. 21-24.

Cook, Robert "Long-lived Seeds." *Natural History*, February 1979, pp. 55-60.

Cook, Robert. "Plant Parenthood." *Natural History*, July 1981, pp. 30-35.

Cook, Robert. "Reproduction by Duplication." *Natural History*, March 1980, pp. 88-93.

Grossman, Mary Louise. "Ours Was a World Without Flowers Until 'Just Recently'." *Smithsonian*, February 1979, pp. 199-130.

WEB SITES

Friends of the Earth
   http://www.foe.co.uk
The Natural History Museum
   http://www.nhm.ac.uk
Royal Botanical Gardens, Kew
   http://www.rbgkew.org.uk
Soil Association
   http://www.soilassociation.org

CONSERVATION ORGANIZATIONS

Audubon Naturalist Society of the Central Atlantic States
8940 Jones Mill Road
Chevy Chase, MD 20815
http://www.audubonnaturalist.org

The Conservation Foundation
1717 Massachusetts Avenue, N.W.
Washington, D.C. 20036
http://www.theconservationfoundation.org

Environmental Defense Fund
257 Park Avenue South, Suite 16
New York, NY 10016
http://www.environmentaldefense.org/home.cfm

National Audubon Society
950 Third Avenue
New York, NY 10022
http://www.audubon.org

National Wildlife Federation
1412 16th Street, N.W.
Washington, D.C. 20036
http://www.nwf.org

World Wildlife Fund
1255 23rd Street, N.W.
Washington, D.C. 20037
http://www.worldwildlife.org

A

Acid rain, 147
Adaptation
    and evolution, 36
    and reproduction, 68
    and survival, 1, 5–7, 9–10, 14, 23–28,
        30–32, 34–35
Adventitious roots, 14
Aerial roots, 14
Aesthetic values, 92, 103–104, 114
    and landscaping, 105–107
Alcohol, 88–89
Algae
    types of, 8, 30–31, 48, 161
Angiosperm, 15, 34
Animal dispersal
    types of, 17, 19, 26–27, 64, 67, 70
Animal habitats
    adaptation, 5, 30
    food sources, 10–11, 43–44, 52, 55,
        62–64, 75–76, 115–116
    plants' effects on, 8, 43, 46, 76, 86,
        92–93, 106, 109–110
Annual plants, 19, 37
Apios priceana, 140
Armstrong, W. P., 65
Artemisia annua, 97
Artic tundra
    vegetation, 5–6, 10, 24, 31
Ash tree, 66
Auxin, 12

B

Backyard conservation
    importance of, 134
    landscaping, 147–150
    snow fences, 150–151
    windbreaks, 151
Bacteria, 31, 51, 55
    effects of, 61, 121
    and nitrogen, 48
    removal of, 56, 97–98
    in water, 80
Banyan tree, 2
Bark, 19, 87, 113, 159
Bedrock, 49
Beech trees, 64, 110
Belladonna, 97
Biodiversity
    benefits of, 2, 57
    defined, 57
    effects on, 60–62, 93, 120, 125–126,
        131, 135, 138–140
    role of, 1–2, 4–6, 11, 30, 34

studies of, 2, 4–5
    and unity, 19–20, 35
Bioengineering, 79
Biofuels
    biodiesel, 107–108
    ethanol, 107
    production, 44, 77, 92, 159
Biogeographers, 70–71
Biomass
    feedstocks, 77, 159
    fuels, 76–77, 88, 159
Biomes
    diverse, 5–6
    influences on, 5
    major, 1, 6–11
Biosynthesis gas, 77
Biotechnology
    breeding, 153
    genetic engineering, 152–156
    hybridization, 153–154
Bluegum trees, 87
Botanical resources. *See* Resources
Botanists
    classification systems, 38–40
    and invasive species, 60–63, 120
    study of biodiversity, 2, 4–5, 34, 60
Botany
    concepts of, 1–29
    economic, 76
Box elder, 66
Bulbs, 84
Burdock plant, 67
Bureau of Land Management, 137, 139
Burs, 19, 26, 67
Buttress roots, 14

C

Cacti, 5, 30, 148
    poaching of, 116, 140
    saguaro, 9–10, 24
    spines, 10, 24
Cambium, 19
Camptotheca acuminata, 97
Canna lily, 110
Carbon cycles, 2, 46, 50
Carbon dioxide, 11
    and photosynthesis, 47
    release of, 76–77, 107, 122, 147,
        151
    sequestrations, 77–78
Carboniferous period, 32
Carnivores, 50, 82, 109
Carnivorous plants, 26–27
Castor bean, 112

Cattail
    products from, 8, 66, 68, 111
Cellulose, 12, 77, 89, 107
Center for Plant Conservation, 139
Cereals, 88
Chicory, 111
Chlorophyll, 8, 12
    function of, 31, 52–53
    and leaves, 15, 105
Cinchona tree, 87
Classification
    binomial nomenclature, 39–40
    groups of, 39
    hierarchical system, 38–39
    of species, 30, 38–40
Climatologists, 29, 82, 138
Clone, 155
Cocklebur, 27
Cola acuminata, 113–114
Combustion, 49
Coniferous forests
    products, 88
    reproduction, 15
    shelter, 85
    species in, 6, 32, 64
Conservation issues
    defined, 135
    education, 141–142
    endangered species, 40–41, 138–146
    habitat loss, 134–135, 137
    and pollution, 146–147
    protection of resources, 93–94, 99,
        137–138, 142, 151, 164
Continental drift, 34, 70–71
Cross-breeding
    discoveries and, 92, 100–101, 103,
        153
Cross-pollination, 17
Curare, 97
Cutting, 21, 154

D
Dandelion
    products from, 111
    and seed dispersal, 19, 65–66
Darwin, Charles, 103
Decay, 11
Deciduous trees, 6, 28, 104
Decomposition, 48, 51
Denitrification, 48
Deserts
    aridity, 10
    and carbon sequestration, 78
    plants of, 5–6, 9–10, 24–25, 159
Devil's claw, 26

Disease, 117
    agents of, 61–62
    cures and treatments with plants, 2, 5,
        87, 93–97, 99–100, 109, 149
    of plants, 4, 19, 115, 117, 153
Dispersal, seed
    animal, 17, 19, 26–27, 64, 67, 70
    effects on, 61
    fire, 64, 68
    mechanical, 64, 67
    mechanisms of, 18, 57, 63–68, 70
    water, 19, 64, 67, 70
    wind, 17, 19, 28, 34, 64–68, 72
Dormant period, 5, 24
    winter, 29, 130
Drift, 34
Duckweed, 1

E
Ecological issues, 92, 114
Ecology, 39, 42, 61
Ecosystem
    abiotic factors, 35
    biotic factors of, 5, 52
    equilibrium, 35, 43, 76, 81, 135,
        138
    niches, 62, 139
    resources, 43, 58, 159
    restoration, 142, 164
    survival in, 20, 40
    threats to, 61, 63, 114, 116, 119, 124,
        129
Elderberry, 111
Elms, 66
Embryo, 19
Endangered plants, 30
    causes, 56, 62, 94, 99, 109, 114, 116
    defined, 138, 143
    laws, 40–41, 140–144
    locations, 71
    and protection, 139, 142–144
    rare, 139, 157
    TESS list, 144–146
    and trends, 40–41, 134, 138–140
Endangered Species Act
    details of, 40–41, 134, 140–144
Endangered Species Conservation Act,
    144
Endangered Species Preservation Act,
    143–144
Endangered and Threatened Wildlife and
    Plants list, 141
Endemic species, 57, 70
    defined, 58, 68, 142
    world regions of, 60, 71–72

Energy, 88
  coal, 32, 43–44, 88
  fuel, 75, 88
  resources, 43–44, 50–52, 76–77, 93,
    159
  storage, 52–53
  wind and water, 43
Environment
  changes in, 20–21, 25, 30–31, 35, 37, 42,
    143, 161
  health, 5, 81
  protection, 134, 137–138
Environmental benefits, 1, 117
  biomass production, 76–77, 88
  carbon sequestration, 77–78
  coastal dune stabilization, 81
  erosion reduction, 78–79
  water quality improvement, 80–81
  wetland restoration, 79–80
Ergot, 97
Ethnobotany
  and American Indian tribes, 72–74,
    87, 94
  contributions, 57
  importance of, 72–74
Ethnoveterinary medicine, 96
Evaporation, 45, 54
Evergreen, 6, 23, 66, 112
Evolution, 7, 30–41
Evotranspiration, 45
Exotic species, 119, 139
Extinction
  prevention, 40, 137, 142
  reasons for, 9, 30, 32, 35–36, 134
  threats of, 40–41, 94, 96, 109, 139–141,
    144, 157

F

Ferns, 6, 11, 106, 148
  coal source, 32, 88
  reproduction, 15
Fertilization, 17
Fibrous roots, 13
Fires
  alterations to, 61, 129
  dispersal, 64, 68
  and erosion, 78
Fish and Wildlife Service, 141, 144
Fleming, Alexander, 97
Floss silk tree, 66
Flowering plants, 17, 106, 167
  adaptation, 35
  in the artic, 10
  classification, 5
  first appearance, 32, 34

  leaves of, 14
  and seed dispersal, 65
Flowers, 1, 39, 159
  blooming, 5
  diversity, 2
  false, 27
  food sources, 84
  growth cycle, 12, 24, 28
  morphology, 15, 17, 20
  nectar, 17, 20, 27, 116
Food
  and biotechnology, 152–153, 159
  chain, 50–52, 76
  consumers, 50, 75, 119, 121
  effects on, 61–63, 109, 115, 119, 149
  and grasses, 10, 44
  and supplements, 82–85, 114, 156
  webs, 43, 50–52, 56, 62–63, 75, 82, 93
  and wilderness survival, 110–112
Forest Service, 137, 139
Fossil
  fuels, 43–44, 88, 159
  research, 34, 36
Fruit plants, 15
  products from, 90, 110
  and seed dispersal, 63, 65–67, 82
Fungi, 50, 55–56, 121
Future issues, 114, 152–165

G

Genetics, 93
  and cross-breeding, 100–101, 103
  engineering, 103, 152–156
  variability, 36, 117, 124
Geographic Information System, 123
Geologic time scale, 33
Geotropism, 12, 21
Germination
  and annual plants, 37
  seed, 5, 18–19, 60, 70, 137, 157
Germplasm, 21, 155–156
Ginseng, 99
Gliders, 65
Global warming, 107
Glucose
  storage, 12, 15, 52–53, 83–85
Goods and Services, 92–93
Goodyear, Charles, 89
Gorse, 67
Gourd family, 65, 97
Grasses, 6, 8, 149
  cheat, 37
  flowers, 15
  and food sources, 10, 44
  and herbicides, 55

Grasses *(continued)*
    root systems, 13–14, 37, 81
    seed dispersal, 67
Grasslands
    destruction of, 134
    plant life in, 10–11, 55
    soil, 11
Gravity, 12, 21, 45
Greenhouse effect, 76
    emissions, 77
    gases, 107
Groundwater
    contamination, 118
    systems, 7, 45, 55, 121
Gymnosperm, 15

H
Habitat, 4, 86
    conservation, 147–150
    destruction and loss, 61, 115–117,
        134–135, 137–139, 144
    diverse, 5–11, 14, 30, 43, 56, 109
    isolated, 58, 68, 70–72, 143
    native, 57–58, 94
    nonnative, 57–58, 75
Hawaii
    ecosystem, 71–72, 117, 138–140,
        143
Heartwood, 29
Helicopters "whirlybirds," 66
Hemicellulose, 89
Hemlock, 66
Herbicide
    function, 55, 129, 147, 157,
        164
Herbivores, 48, 50, 82, 109–110
Hevea brasiliensis, 149
Hickories, 64
History
    and plants' roles, 74–75, 92, 100,
        112–114
Honey guides, 20
Hormones, 155
Horsetails, 88
Horticulturalists, 82
Host plant, 117, 119
Humans' role
    effects on wetlands, 9
    and the environment, 35, 40, 42–43,
        55–56, 58, 60, 90, 118, 125, 134–135,
        139, 141, 147–151, 164–165
    and the food chain, 52, 75–76, 82
    public awareness, 57, 62–63, 142
    and urbanization, 56, 139
Hydrotropism, 21

I
Importance, 115
    aesthetic benefits, 103–107, 114
    biofuels, 107–108
    genetics, 100–101, 103
    goods and services, 92–93
    medicinal resources, 43, 75–76, 93–100,
        112, 114, 119
    recreational, 108–110, 114
Industrial products
    clothing, 75, 86–87
    plant productions, 44, 88–90
    and recycling, 89
Insect
    diversity, 35, 43
    effects on, 61–62
    and pesticides, 55–56
Inspirational values, 44, 90–91
Interior Department's Fish and Wildlife
    Service, 40
International Code of Botanical Nomen-
    clature, 39
Introduced species, 57
Invasive activities, 137
Invasive species
    defined, 58
    hybrids, 61, 103, 153–154
    impact of, 57–58, 60–63, 120–121
    weeds, 44, 115, 124–131, 157
Inventory, 57, 62–63
Isolated Species, 68, 70–71

J
Juniper, 111

K
Kapok tree, 66

L
Land management
    planning issues, 115, 119–121
    poor practices, 139
Leaves, 8
    chloroplasts, 15, 52–53
    cuticle, 14
    diversity, 2, 14
    epidermis, 14
    growth cycle, 1, 12, 19, 21, 28
    functions, 14–15, 20–21, 23–24, 26–27,
        31, 45, 52, 54–55, 83–84, 105
    layers, 14–15
    palisade cell, 15
    stomata, 15, 24, 53
Legumes, 66–67
Lianas, 11

Lichen
    types of, 6, 10, 48, 161
Life cycles
    of plants, 1, 11–19
    yearly, 28–29
Lignin, 89
Linnaeus, Carolus
    Species Plantarum, 39
Loofah, 90
Lupines, 67

M

Madagascar periwinkle, 97
Management
    disease, 117
    exotic species, 119
    habitat destruction, 115–17
    land use, 119–121
    overexploitation, 118
    poisonous plants, 131–133
    pollution, 118
    soil management, 121–124
    weeds, 124–131
Mangrove, 14
Maples, 66
Marsh violet, 8
Masting, 63–64
Mayapple, 97
Mechanical dispersal, 64, 67
Medicine and healthcare, 119
    aromatherapy, 98–100
    herbal, 43, 85, 87, 93–96, 99–100
    and plants, 74–76, 92–100,
        148–149
    prescription, 43, 87, 94, 96–98, 112
Meiosis, 103
Mendel, Gregor, 101, 103
Mestral, George de, 27
Mesozoic era, 32
Milkweed, 66
Mineralization, 47
Molecule, 15
Monitoring
    role of, 57, 62–63, 117–118, 137
Moss
    club, 32
    locations, 6, 8, 10
    peat, 8, 79, 123
    reproduction, 31
Mulches, 123

N

Native species
    effects on, 57–58, 60–62, 72, 94, 119,
        126–127, 129, 131

and landscaping, 120
    rare, 139
Natural Resources Conservation Service,
    138, 151
Natural selection, 35–36
Nitrification, 48
Nitrogen cycle, 2, 47–48, 50
Nixon, Richard, 144

O

Oak tree, 64, 111, 113, 148
Oceans
    and carbon sequestration, 78
    expansion, 34
    plants near, 5, 47
    primitive plants in, 31
Opium poppies, 87, 97
Orchids, 11, 23, 65, 140
Organ, 20
Organism, 19
    habitats, 49
    interrelationships of, 20–21, 35, 51, 56
Osmosis, 15
Outer space
    plant experiments in, 152, 161–164
Overexploitation, 115, 118
    and collecting, 139–140
Oxygen cycle, 49

P

Paleocene epoch, 35
Paleoclimatologists, 82
Palm trees, 30, 148
    coconut, 23, 67, 70, 85
    oils, 88, 90, 159
Parasite, 26
Penicillin, 97–98
Perennial plants, 19, 37
Pesticides
    effects of, 55–56, 121, 153
Phenol, 77
Phloem, 12, 19, 34
Photosynthesis
    and carbon dioxide, 47
    and oxygen, 31–32, 43, 49, 53, 76
    process of, 12, 15, 20, 23, 31, 52–55, 105
    and winter, 24
Phototropism, 21
Pigment, 12
Pitcher plants, 140
Poisonous plants
    checklist, 133
    and invasive species, 61, 115, 131–133
    nettles, 26
    weeds, 124–125, 129

Pollen grains, 68
Pollination, 17
    aid in, 20, 28, 56
    effects on, 61–62, 116
Pollution
    air, 147, 161
    effects of, 115, 118, 134, 139, 146–147
    filtering of, 50
    soil, 79, 81, 118, 146
    water, 9, 79–81, 118, 129, 135, 146, 161
Pondweed, 8
Population potential, 65
Primitive plants, 30–32, 34
Protein, 48
Purple foxglove, 97

R

Raffia palms, 2
Rain forest
    biodiversity in, 5–6, 14, 24, 43, 82, 135
    climate, 6
    destruction of, 5, 116, 134–135, 138
    layers of, 6, 23
Recreational, 93, 108–110, 114
Redwood trees, 2, 30
Reeds, 8
Reproduction
    and seeds, 15, 17, 19, 60, 68
    types of, 31, 34
Research and discovery, 152–165
    on biodiversity, 2, 4–5, 110
    on biofuels, 77, 107–108
    biotechnology, 152–156
    on carbon sinks, 78
    on cross-breeding, 100–101, 103
    and disease, 2, 93–98
    on endangered species, 40–41, 118, 141
    on isolated species, 70–72
    on invasive species, 60–63, 124–125,
        129, 131
    on primitive plants, 31, 34, 36
    on resources, 42, 82, 88, 93, 114, 148
    on soil, 123–124
Resources
    development of, 57–74
    management, 36, 42, 115–120, 124,
        134–135, 137
    nonrenewable, 42–43, 49, 52
    renewable, 42–44, 52
    uses of, 43, 75–91, 135
Resource cycles, 42, 55
    carbon, 2, 46–48
    nitrogen, 2, 36, 48
    oxygen, 49
    water, 43, 45–46, 76

Respiration
    process of, 14, 47, 49, 52–55
    rate, 54–55
Rhizome, 14
Roots, 2, 8–9
    functions, 12–13, 21, 29, 31, 43, 52, 55,
        78–79, 104
    and gravity, 21
    growth cycle, 12, 24, 31
    protection of, 14, 25–26, 48, 50, 52
    types of, 13–14, 37
Rosebush, 26, 90
Rose hips, 87
Rushes, 8

S

Sagebrush, 10
Saltbush, 66
Sapwood, 29
Seashores
    coastal dune stabilization, 81, 139
    vegetation of, 7, 31–32, 81
Seed banks, 137, 152, 157
Seedling, 1, 62–63, 157
Seeds
    dispersal, 17–19, 26–28, 34, 57, 61,
        63–68, 70
    dormant, 5, 130
    germination, 5, 18–19, 60, 70, 137, 157
    primitive, 32, 34
    production, 17–18, 24, 28, 63–64
    and reproduction, 15, 17, 60
    sprouting, 1
Senna alexandrina, 97
Sequoias, 1–2, 30
Sexual reproduction
    examples of, 31
Shelter, 127
    from plants, 43, 75–76, 85–87, 121, 149
Shrubs, 6, 81, 106
    flowers, 15
    products from, 111, 149
Soil
    effects on, 62, 121–124
    erosion, 46, 49, 56, 61–62, 78–79, 118,
        121, 123, 129, 138, 147, 159, 164–165
    fertility, 49, 121–123, 125
    and the food chain, 52
    formation, 2, 49–50
    functions, 50, 52, 55
    management, 115, 121–124
    pollutants, 79, 81, 118, 146
    resources, 49–50
    types of, 49–50
Species Plantarum (Linnaeus), 39

Starch, 77
  edible, 110
  storage, 12–13, 53, 83
Stem, 8
  functions, 13–14, 20, 31, 84
  growth cycle, 12, 19, 21, 31
  primitive plants, 32
  production, 1
Stinging nettle, 26
Stone plants, 28
Succession, 36–38
Succulent, 9
Sundew, 26
Survival
  in artic, 10
  in deserts, 9–10
  mechanisms of, 1, 5–7, 14, 19–21,
    23–28, 35
Sycamore, 66

T

Taproots, 7, 13
Taxonomy, 38, 40
Temperate forests, 6
TESS list, 144–146
Textile plants, 152
Thigmotropism, 21
Topiary, 106
Topography, 49
Track synthesis, 71
Transpiration
  process of, 10, 14, 43, 45, 52–55, 76, 104
Trichosanthes kirilowii, 97
Tropics
  plant life in, 11, 23
  products from, 89, 110, 113, 116
Tropism
  types of, 20–21, 23
Tubers, 83–84
Tulips, 19, 90
Tumbleweeds, 66

U

United States Commerce Department's
    National Oceanic and Atmospheric
    Administration, 41
Uses
  energy, 88
  environmental, 76–81
  food and supplements, 44, 50–52,
    61–63, 75–76, 82–85, 121, 149
  industrial, 32, 75, 86–90
  inspirational, 44, 90–91
  medicine and health care, 43, 75–76, 87,
    93–100, 112, 114, 119, 148–149

  scientific applications, 82
  shelter, 43, 75–76, 85–87, 121, 127, 149

V

Vascular plant, 72
Vegetables, 82–83
Velcro, 27
Venus fly trap, 26
Vicariance distribution, 70–71
Victoria water lily, 2
Vines, 15, 23, 66
Virus, 61, 117
Volcanic eruption
  effects on the environment, 36, 49, 72,
    135
Vulcanization, 89

W

Water
  bodies, 8, 81
  conservation, 147, 161
  cycles, 43, 45–46, 50, 76
  dispersal, 19, 64, 67, 70
  pollutants, 79–81, 118, 129, 135, 146, 161
  power, 43
  quality improvement, 80–81, 118, 163
  storage, 79
  table, 55, 146
Water lily, 67
Weeds
  facts, 126–27
  and herbicides, 55–56, 129, 157
  invasive, 44, 115, 124–131, 157
  multiply, 128
  noxious, 124–125, 129
  spread of, 125–126, 157
  types of, 126–131
Wetlands
  destruction of, 9, 36, 134–135
  restorations, 78–80
  transitional, 8–9
Wilderness
  protection, 134, 137–138
  survival, 92, 110–112
Willows, 66, 87
Wind
  dispersal, 17, 19, 34, 64–68, 72
  power, 43
  types, 65–66

X

Xylem, 12, 19, 34, 113

Y

Yew tree, 97

ABOUT THE AUTHOR

JULIE KERR CASPER holds B.S., M.S., and Ph.D. degrees in earth science with an emphasis on natural resource conservation. She has worked for the United States Bureau of Land Management (BLM) for nearly 30 years and is primarily focused on practical issues concerning the promotion of a healthier, better-managed environment for both the short- and long-term. She has also had extensive experience teaching middle school and high school students over the past 20 years. She has taught classes, instructed workshops, given presentations, and led field trips and science application exercises. She is the author of several award-winning novels, articles, and stories.